ISBN 978-1-4803-9484-1

7777 W. Bluemound Rd. P.O. Box 13819 Milwaukee, WI 53213

Visit Hal Leonard Online at
www.halleonard.com
www.chordbuddy.com

All Shook Up

Words and Music by Otis Blackwell and Elvis Presley

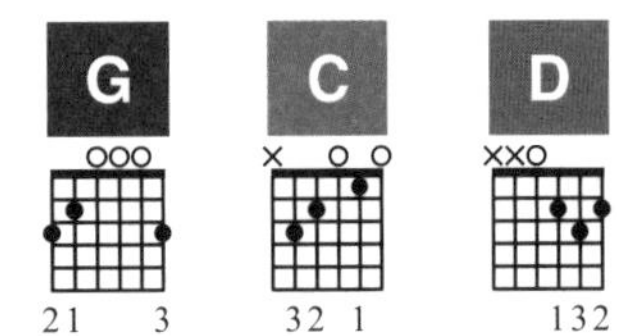

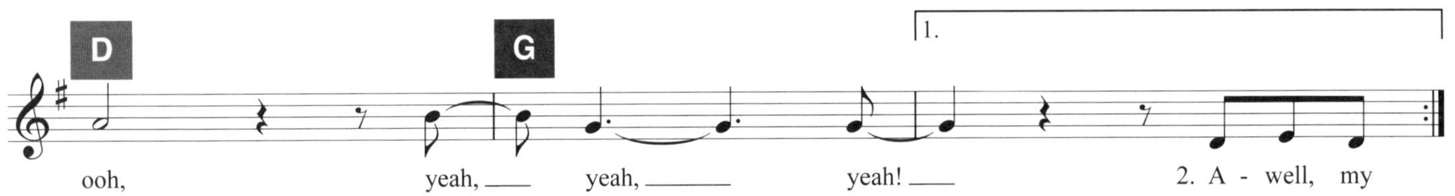

Additional Lyrics

2. A-well, my hands are shaky and my knees are weak,
I can't seem to stand on my own two feet.
Who do you thank when you have such luck?
I'm in love! I'm all shook up! Mm, mm, ooh, ooh, yeah, yeah, yeah!

Bridge: My tongue gets tied when I try to speak.
My insides shake like a leaf on a tree.
There's only one cure for this soul of mine.
That's to have the girl that I love so fine!

Amazing Grace

Words by John Newton
Traditional American Melody

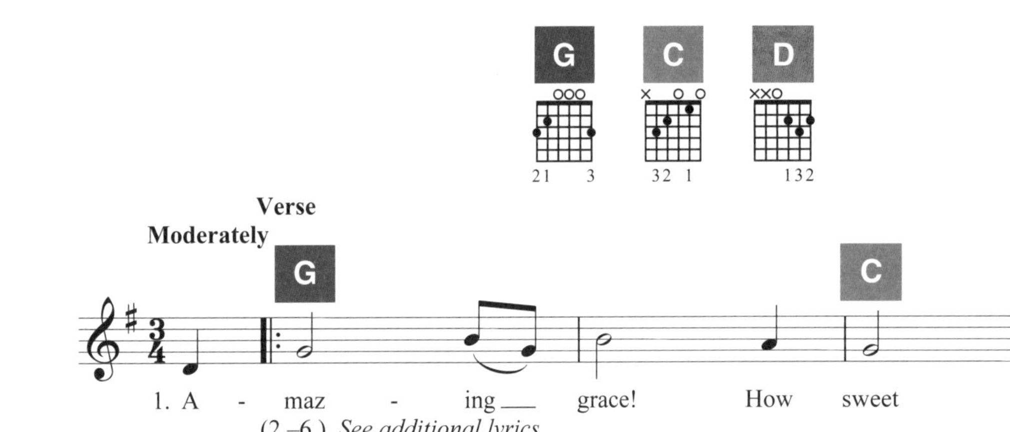

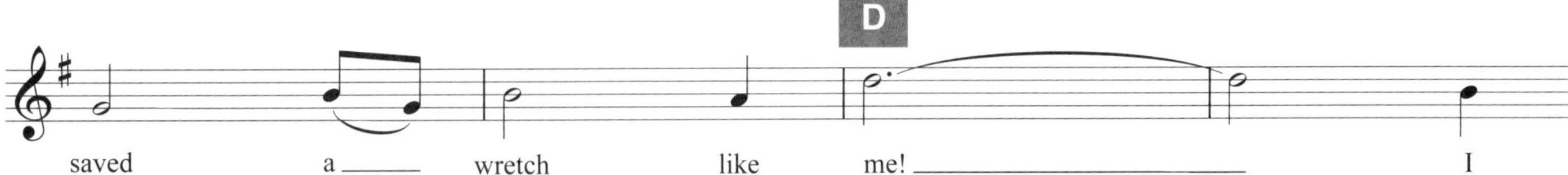

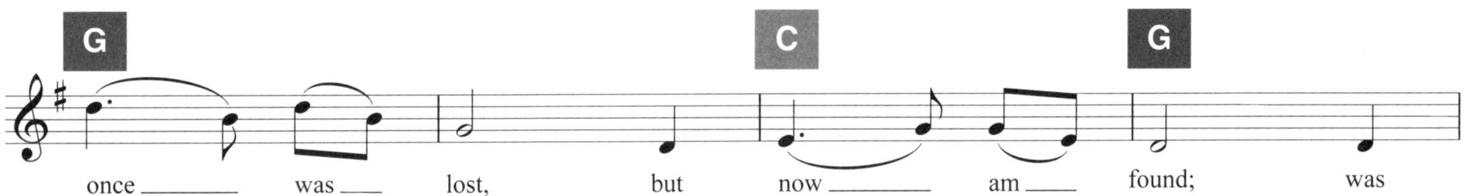

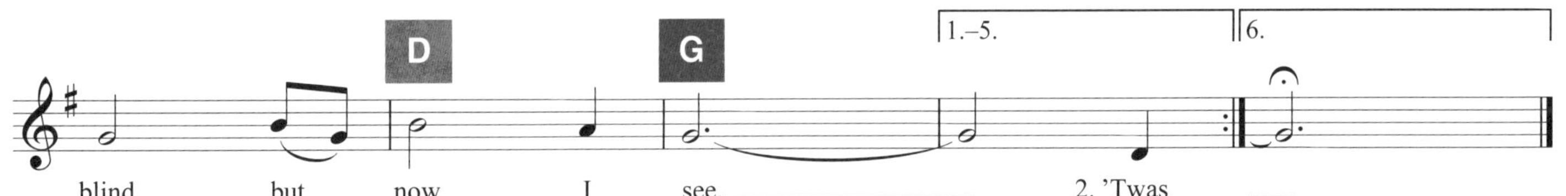

Additional Lyrics

2. 'Twas grace that taught my heart to fear,
   And grace my fears relieved.
   How precious did that grace appear
   The hour I first believed.

3. Through many dangers, toils and snares,
   I have already come.
   'Tis grace hath brought me safe thus far,
   And grace will lead me home.

4. The Lord has promised good to me,
   His word my hope secures.
   He will my shield and portion be
   As long as life endures.

5. And when this flesh and heart shall fail,
   And mortal life shall cease,
   I shall possess within the veil
   A life of joy and peace.

6. When we've been there ten thousand years,
   Bright shining as the sun,
   We've no less days to sing God's praise
   Than when we first begun.

Bad Moon Rising

Words and Music by John Fogerty

Additional Lyrics

2. I hear hurricanes a-blowin'.
   I know the end is comin' soon.
   I fear rivers overflowin'.
   I hear the voice of rage and ruin.

3. Hope you got your things together.
   Hope you are quite prepared to die.
   Looks like we're in for nasty weather.
   One eye is taken for an eye.

Battle Hymn of the Republic

Words by Julia Ward Howe
Music by William Steffe

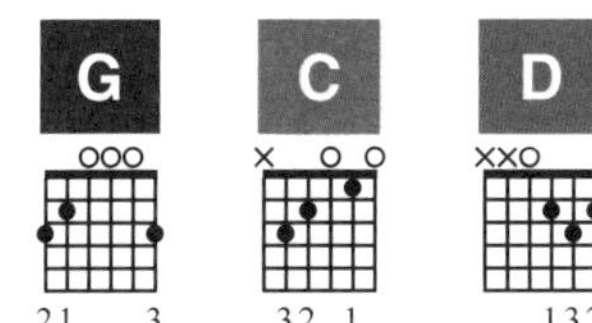

Verse
Bright March

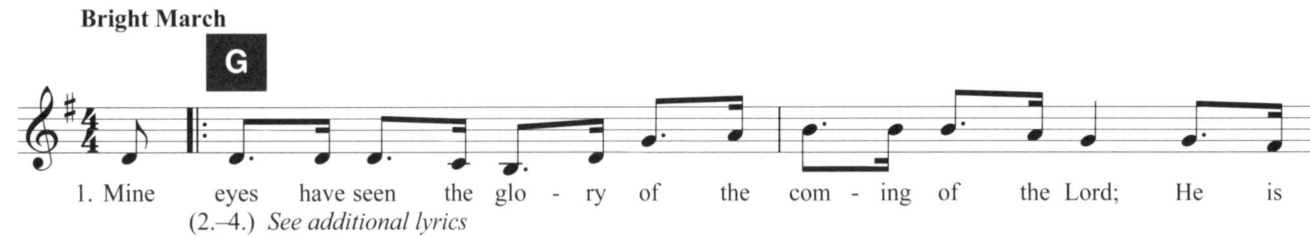

1. Mine eyes have seen the glo - ry of the com - ing of the Lord; He is
(2.–4.) *See additional lyrics*

tram - pling out the vin - tage where the grapes of wrath are stored. He hath loosed the fate - ful light - ning of His

Chorus

C D G G

ter - ri - ble swift sword; His truth is march - ing on. Glo - ry, glo - ry, hal - le-

lu - jah! Glo - ry, glo - ry, hal - le - lu - jah! Glo - ry, glo - ry, hal - le-

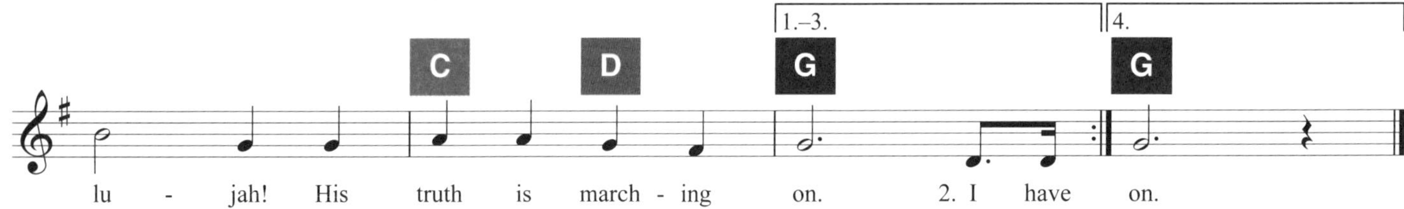

lu - jah! His truth is march - ing on. 2. I have on.

Additional Lyrics

2. I have seen Him in the watchfires of a hundred circling camps;
   They have builded Him an altar in the evening dews and damps.
   I can read His righteous sentence by the dim and flaring lamps;
   His day is marching on.

3. He has sounded forth the trumpet that shall never sound retreat;
   He is sifting out the hearts of men before His judgment seat.
   O be swift, my soul, to answer Him! Be jubilant, my feet!
   Our God is marching on.

4. In the beauty of the lilies Christ was born across the sea,
   With a glory in His bosom that transfigures you and me.
   As He died to make men holy, let us die to make men free,
   While God is marching on.

Busted

Words and Music by Harlan Howard

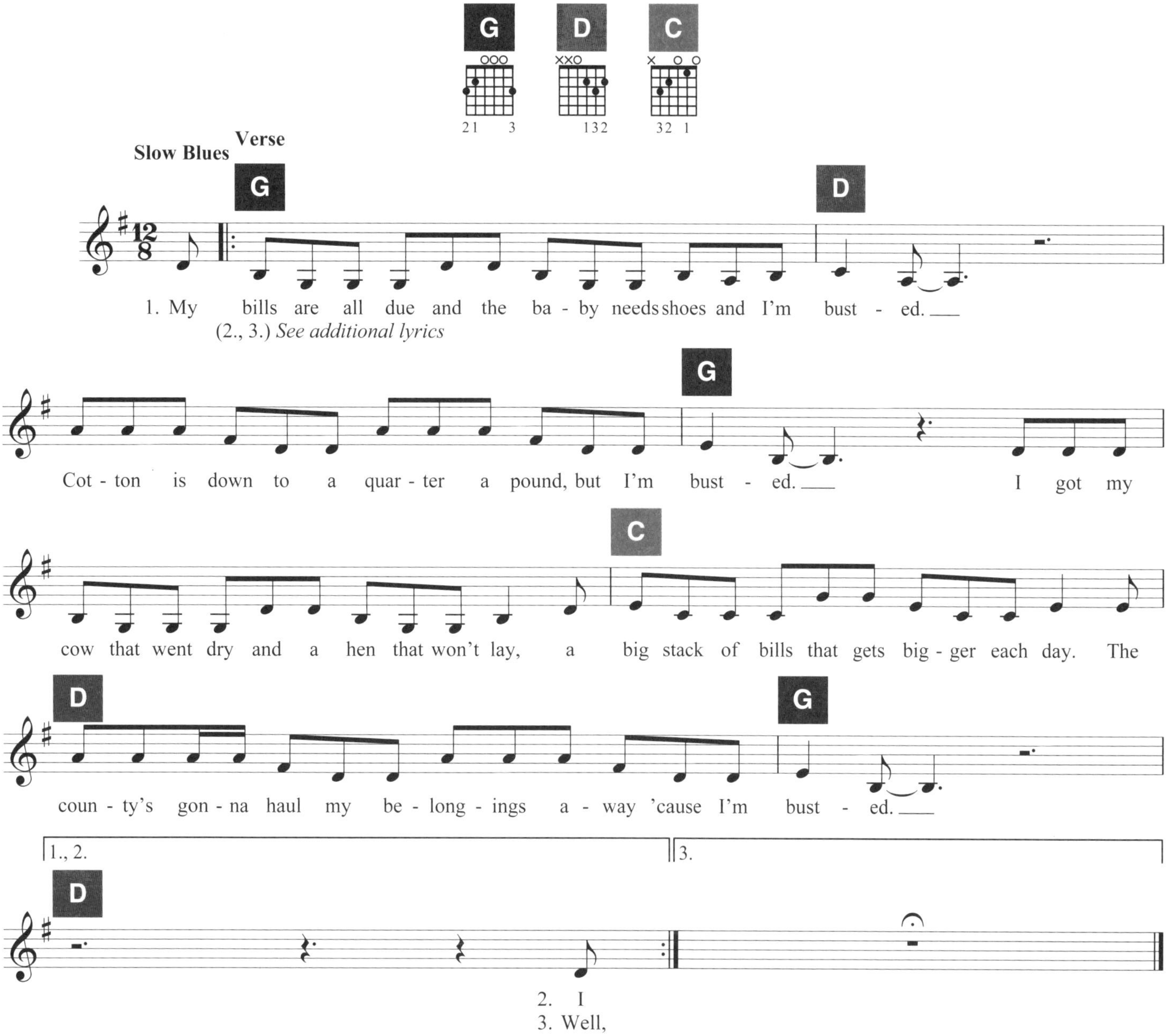
G D C
21 3
132
32 1
Slow Blues
Verse
G
D
1. My bills are all due and the ba - by needs shoes and I'm bust - ed.
(2., 3.) See additional lyrics
G
Cot - ton is down to a quar - ter a pound, but I'm bust - ed. I got my
C
cow that went dry and a hen that won't lay, a big stack of bills that gets big - ger each day. The
D
G
coun - ty's gon - na haul my be - long - ings a - way 'cause I'm bust - ed.
1., 2.
3.
D
2. I
3. Well,

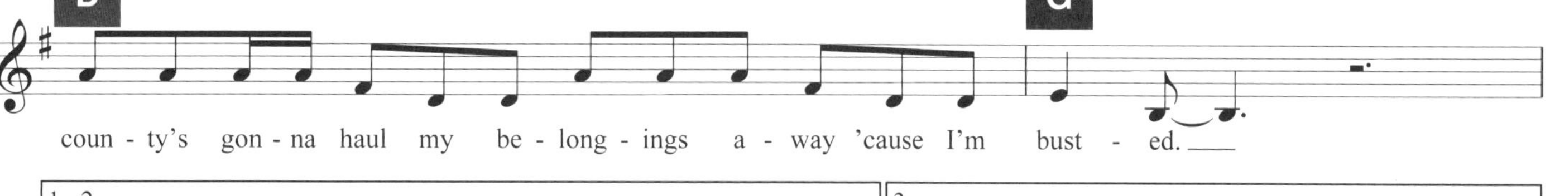

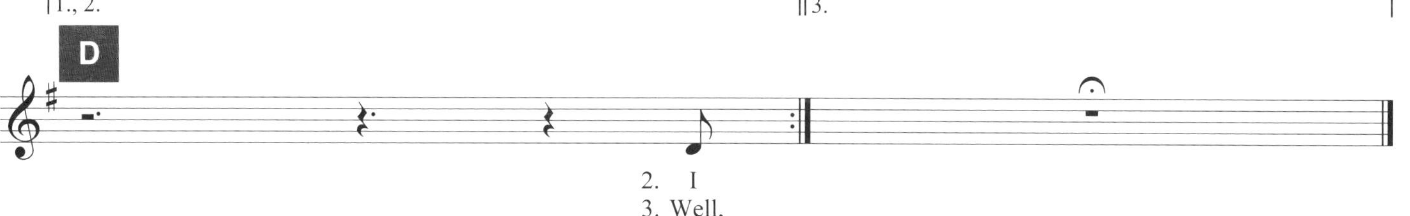

Additional Lyrics

2. I went to my brother to ask for a loan 'cause I was busted.
   I hate to beg like a dog without his bone, but I'm busted.
   My brother said, "There ain't a thing I can do;
   My wife and my kids are all down with the flu,
   And I was just thinking about calling on you! And I'm busted."

3. Well, I am no thief, but a man can go wrong when he's busted.
   The food that we canned last summer is gone and I'm busted.
   The fields are all bare and the cotton won't grow.
   Me and my fam'ly got to pack up and go,
   But I'll make a living, just where I don't know, 'cause I'm busted.

Blue Suede Shoes

Words and Music by Carl Lee Perkins

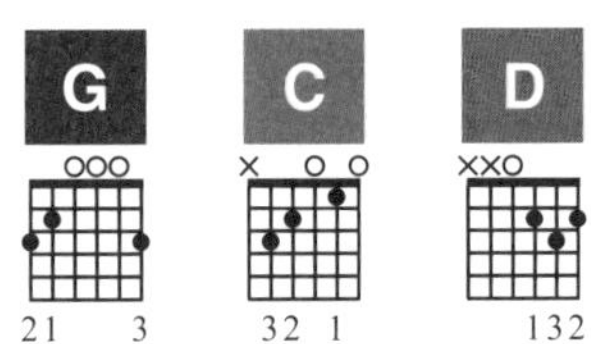

𝄋 Verse

Bright Country Shuffle (♫ = ♩♪ triplet)

N.C. G N.C. G N.C.

1., 4. Well, it's one for the mon-ey, two for the show, three to get read-y, now

G C

go, {cat, / go,} go, but don't ___ you ___ step on my blue suede

G D

shoes. Well, you can do an-y-thing ___ but lay

G *To Coda* 𝄌

off of my blue ___ suede shoes. 2. Well, you can

Verse

G N.C. G N.C. G N.C. G

knock me down, _ step in my face, ___ slan-der my name all
(3.) burn my house, _ steal my car, ___ drink my li-quor from an

N.C. G N.C. G N.C. G

o-ver the place. _ } Well, do an-y-thing ___ that you wan-na do, ___ but
old fruit jar. ___ }

N.C.
G
C
uh - uh, hon - ey, lay off them shoes and don't you
G
D
step on my blue suede shoes. Well, you can do an - y - thing, but lay
G
1.
off of my blue suede shoes. 3. Well, you can
2.
D.S. al Coda
4. Well, it's a -
Coda
Outro
G
Well, it's blue, blue,
C
blue suede shoes, blue, blue, blue suede shoes, yeah, blue, blue,
G
blue suede shoes, ba - by, blue, blue, blue suede shoes. Well, you can
D
G
do an - y - thing but lay off of my blue suede shoes.

Brown Eyed Girl

Words and Music by Van Morrison

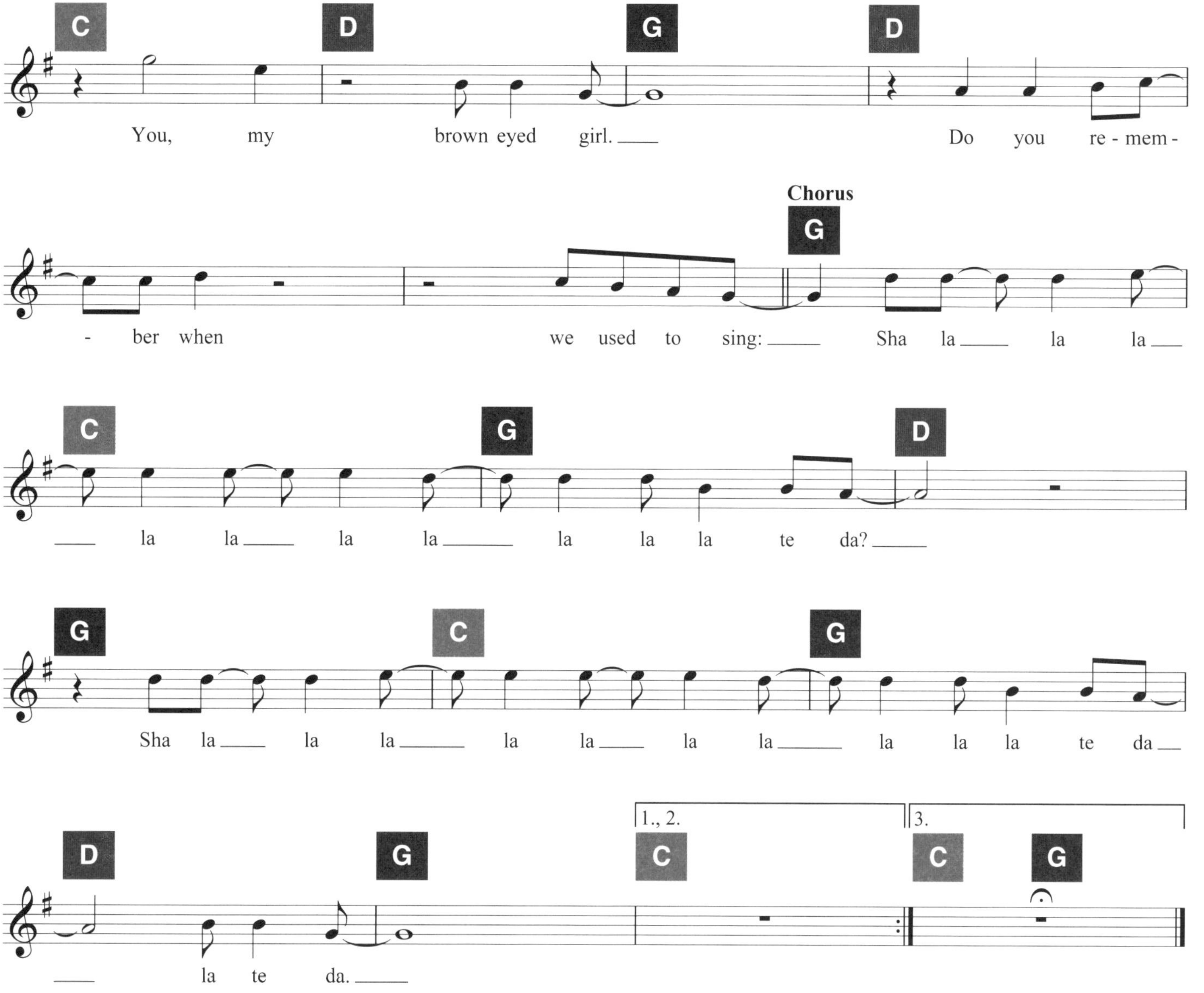

Additional Lyrics

2. Whatever happened to Tuesday and so slow
   Going down the old mine with a transistor radio
   Standing in the sunlight laughing
   Hiding behind a rainbow's wall
   Slipping and a-sliding
   All along the waterfall
   With you, my brown eyed girl,
   You, my brown eyed girl?
   Do you remember when we used to sing:

3. So hard to find my way, now that I'm all on my own
   I saw you just the other day, my, how you have grown
   Cast my memory back there, Lord
   Sometime I'm overcome thinking 'bout
   Making love in the green grass
   Behind the stadium
   With you, my brown eyed girl
   With you, my brown eyed girl.
   Do you remember when we used to sing:

Bye Bye Love

Words and Music by Felice Bryant and Boudleaux Bryant

(Oh, My Darling) Clementine

Words and Music by Percy Montrose

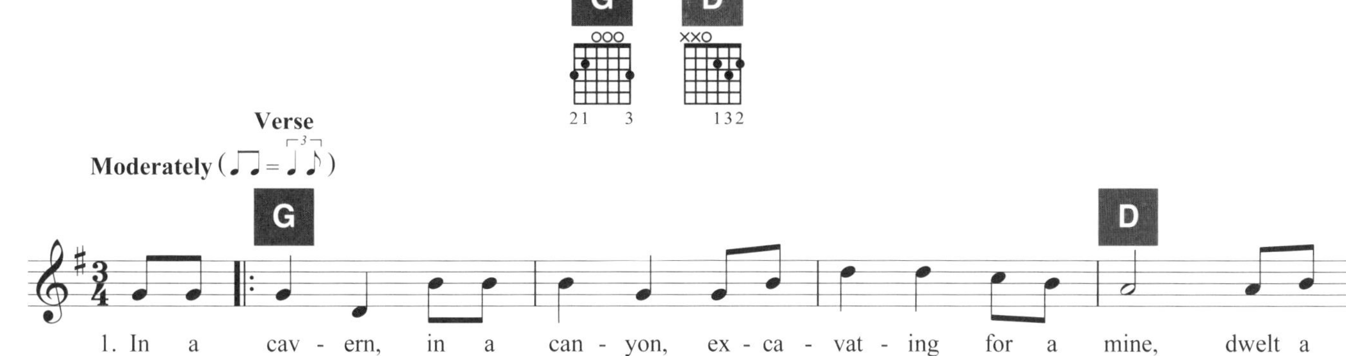

Additional Lyrics

2. Light she was and like a fairy
   And her shoes were number nine,
   Herring boxes, without topses
   Sandals were for Clementine.

3. Drove she ducklings to the water
   Ev'ry morning just at nine,
   Stubbed her toe upon a splinter
   Fell into the foaming brine.

4. Ruby lips above the water
   Blowing bubbles soft and fine,
   But alas I was no swimmer
   So I lost my Clementine.

5. There's a churchyard on the hillside
   Where the flowers grow and twine,
   There grow roses 'mongst the posies
   Fertilized by Clementine.

Cold, Cold Heart

Words and Music by Hank Williams

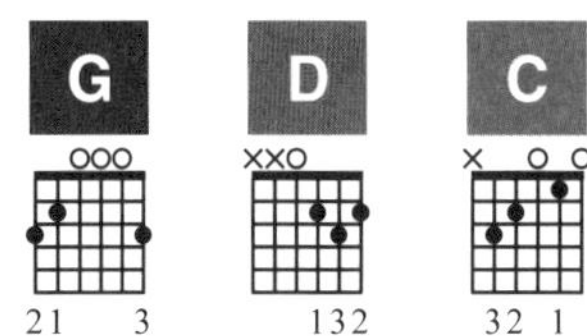

Verse
G
G
heart? 2. An - oth - er love be - fore my time made your heart sad and
heart? 4. There was a time when I be - lieved that you be - longed to

D
blue. And so my heart is pay - ing now for things I did - n't
me. But now I know your heart is shack - led to a mem - o -

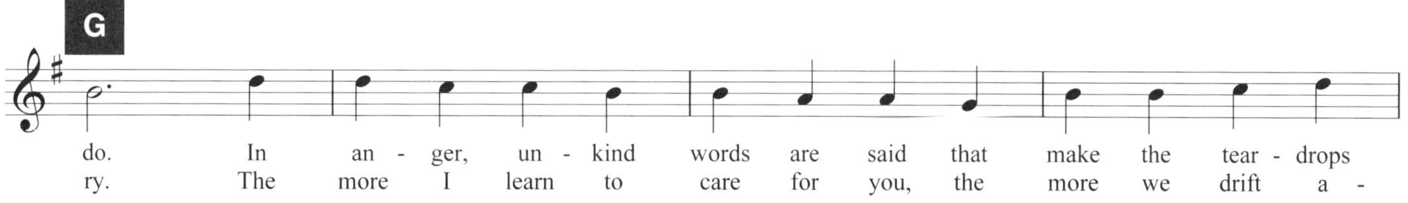
G
do. In an - ger, un - kind words are said that make the tear - drops
ry. The more I learn to care for you, the more we drift a -

C
D
start. Why can't I free your doubt - ful mind and
part. Why can't I free your doubt - ful mind and

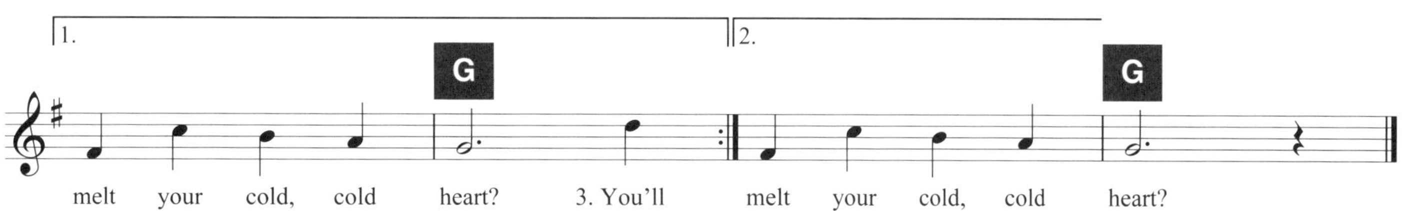
1.
2.
G
G
melt your cold, cold heart? 3. You'll melt your cold, cold heart?

Daddy Sang Bass

Words and Music by Carl Perkins

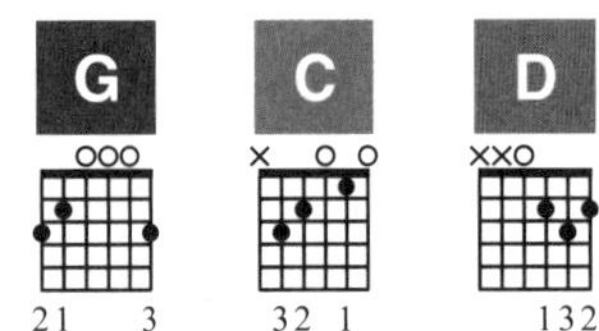

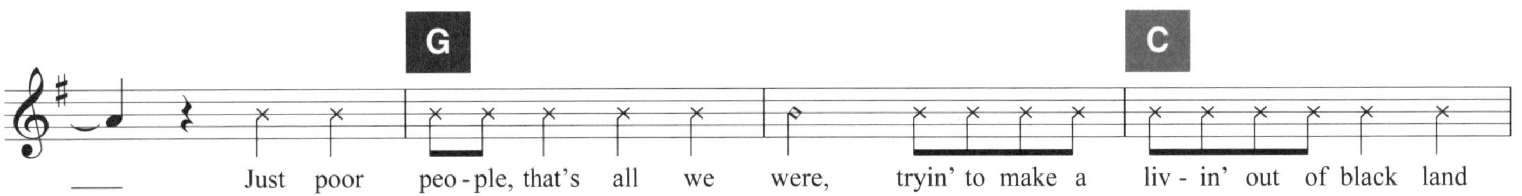

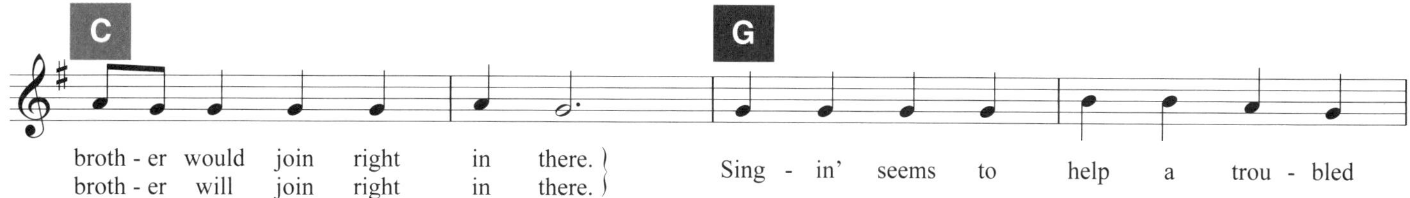
C
G
broth - er would join right in there.
broth - er will join right in there.
Sing - in' seems to help a trou - bled

D
G
soul.
One of these days, and it won't be long, I'll re -

C
G
D
join them in a song. I'm gon - na join the fam - 'ly cir - cle at the

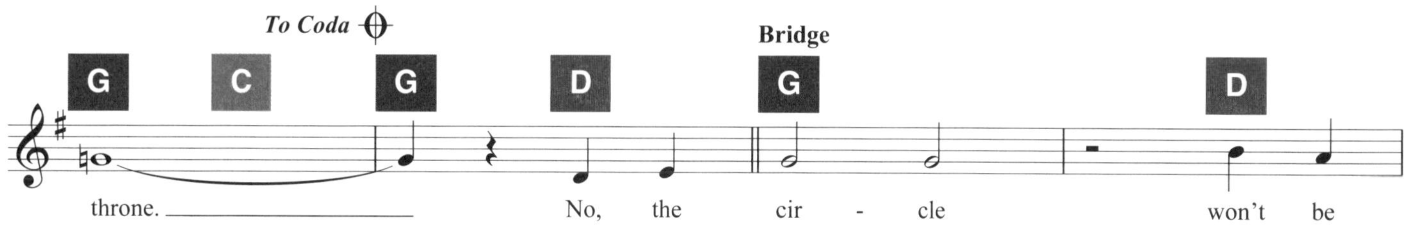
To Coda
Bridge
G
C
G
D
G
D
throne.
No, the cir - cle won't be

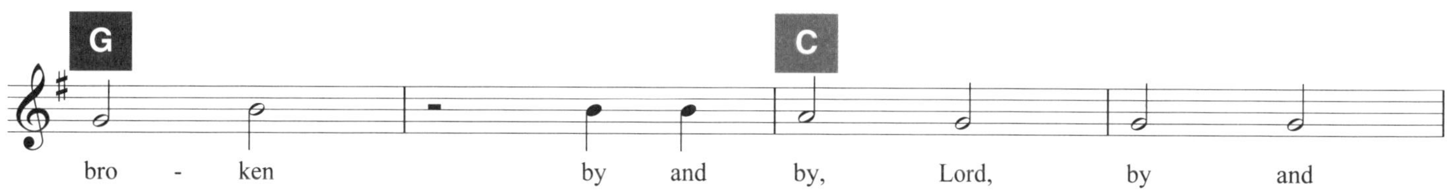
G
C
bro - ken by and by, Lord, by and

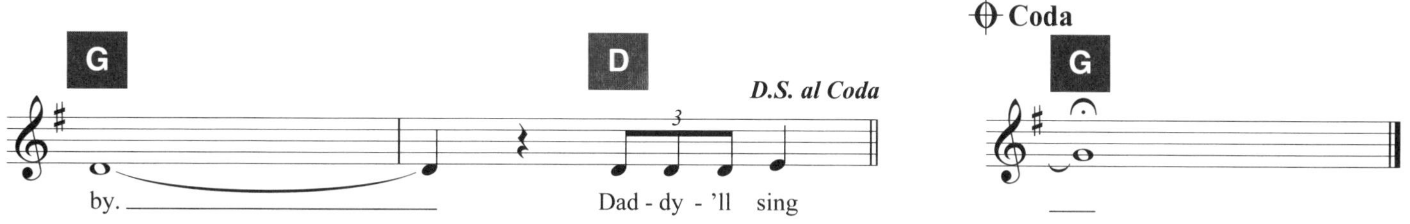
G
D
D.S. al Coda
3
by.
Dad - dy - 'll sing
Coda
G

Do Wah Diddy Diddy

Words and Music by Jeff Barry and Ellie Greenwich

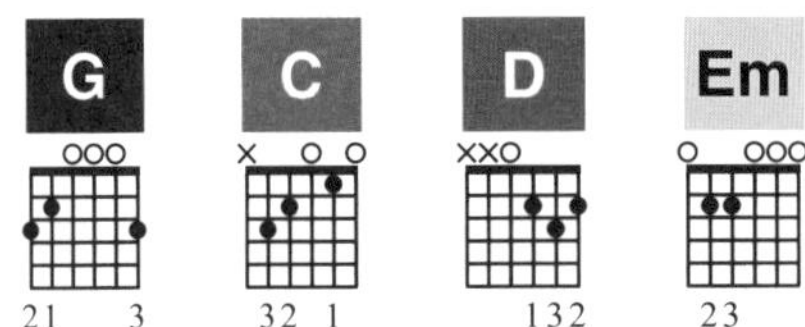

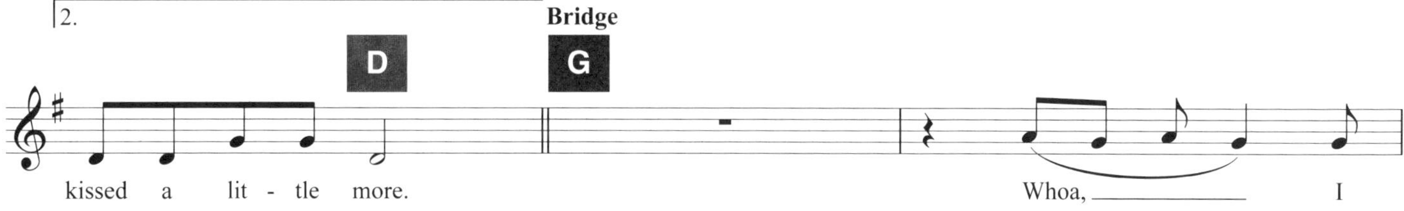

Additional Lyrics

2. Before I knew it, she was walkin' next to me, singin':
   Do wah diddy diddy dum diddy do.
   Holdin' my hand just as natural as can be, singin':
   Do wah diddy diddy dum diddy do.
   We walked on (walked on) to my door (my door).
   We walked on to my door, then we kissed a little more.

3. Now we're together nearly ev'ry single day, singin':
   Do wah diddy diddy dum diddy do.
   We're so happy and that's how we're gonna stay, singin':
   Do wah diddy diddy dum diddy do.
   Well, I'm hers (I'm hers), she's mine (she's mine).
   I'm hers, she's mine; wedding bells are gonna chime.

Down by the Riverside

African-American Spiritual

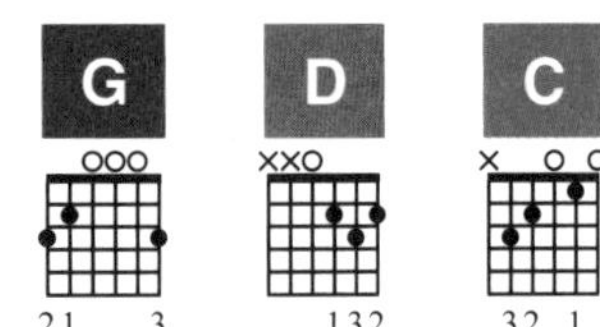

Verse

Rhythmically, in 2

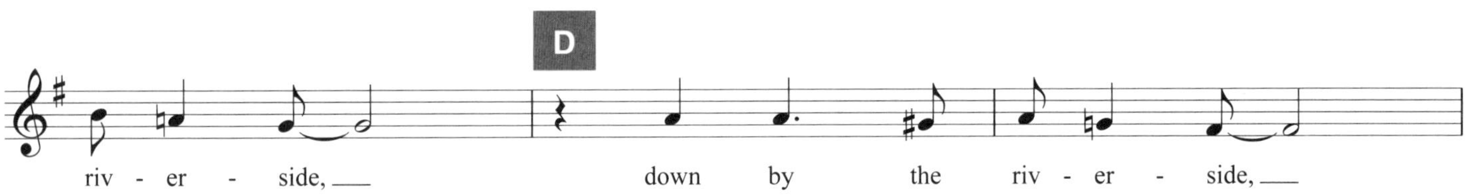

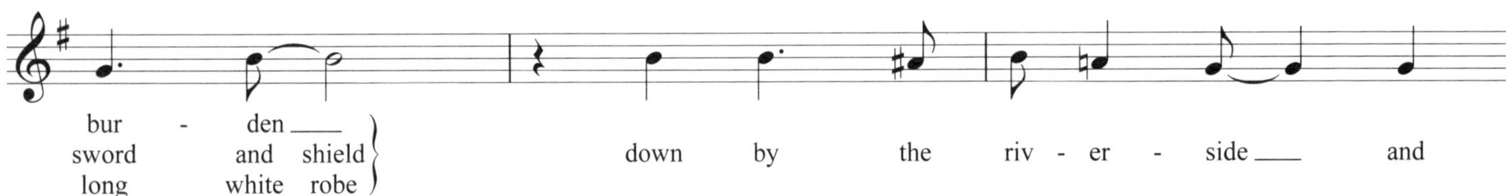

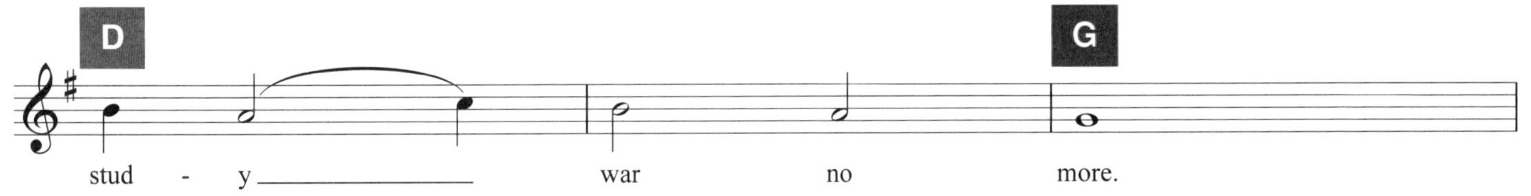

Chorus

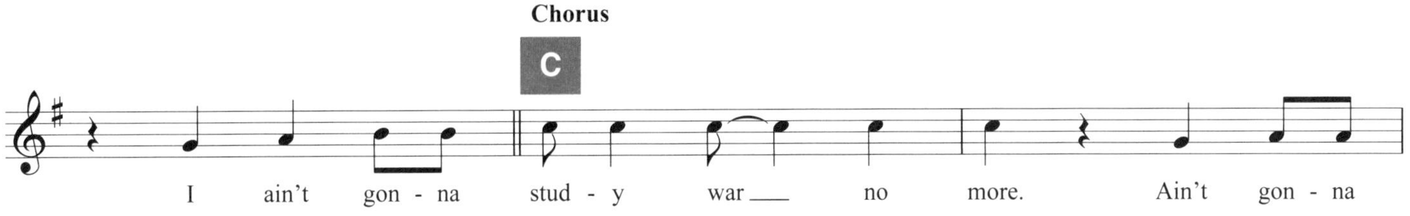
C
I ain't gon - na stud - y war no more. Ain't gon - na

G
D
stud - y war no more. Ain't gon - na stud - y

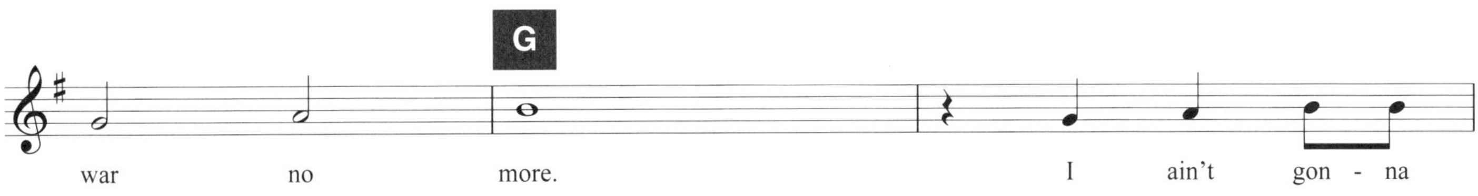
G
war no more. I ain't gon - na

C
G
stud - y war no more. Ain't gon - na stud - y war no

D
more. Ain't gon - na stud - y war no

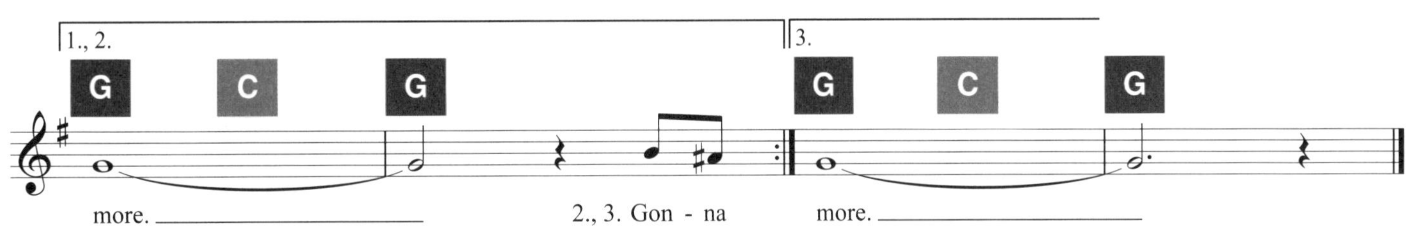
1., 2.
3.
G C G
G C G
more. 2., 3. Gon - na more.

Down on the Corner

Words and Music by John Fogerty

Folsom Prison Blues

Words and Music by John R. Cash

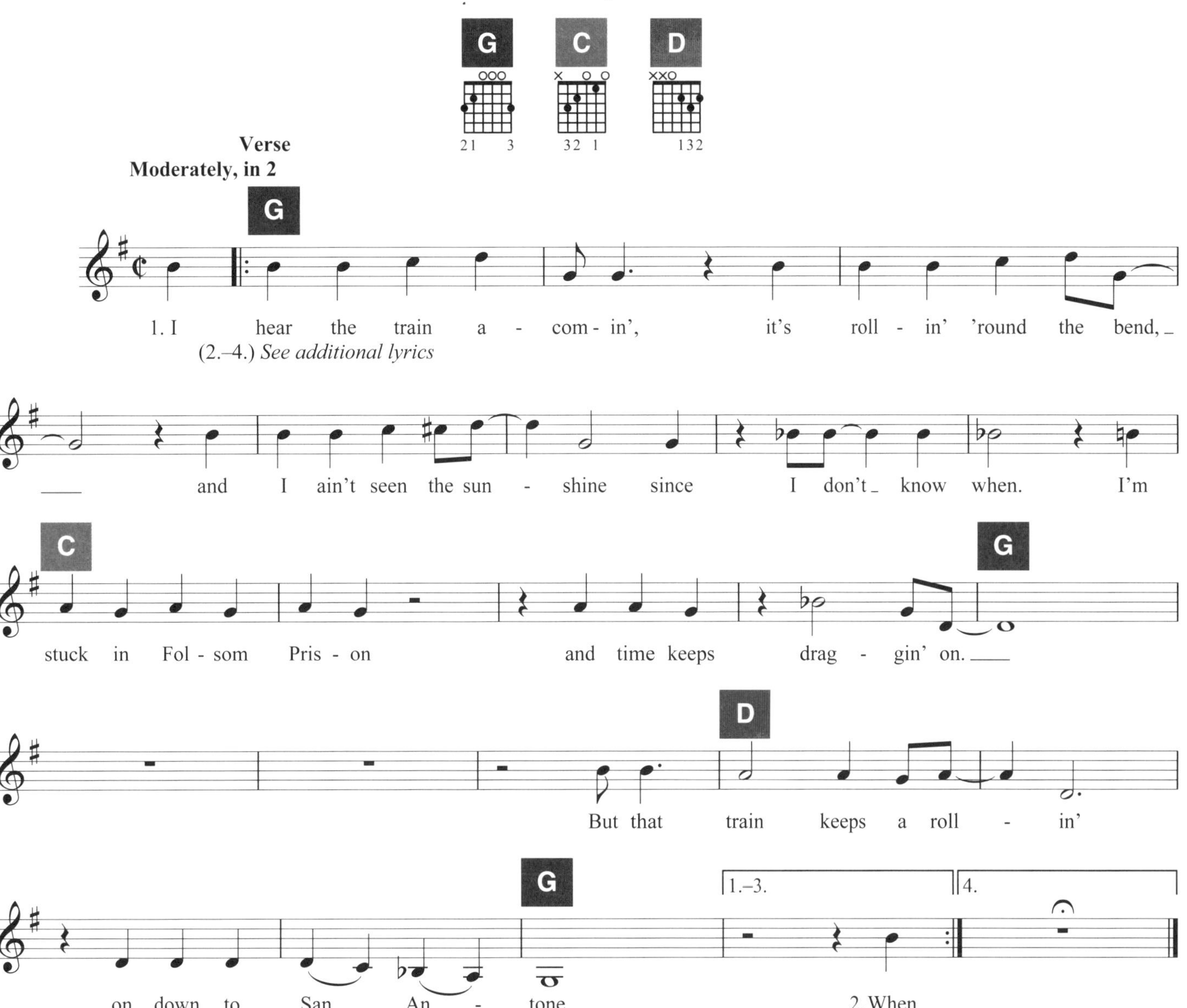

Additional Lyrics

2. When I was just a baby, my mama told me, "Son,
   Always be a good boy; don't ever play with guns."
   But I shot a man in Reno, just to watch him die.
   When I hear that whistle blowin', I hang my head and cry.

3. I bet there's rich folks eatin' in a fancy dining car.
   They're prob'ly drinkin' coffee and smokin' big cigars.
   Well, I know I had it comin', I know I can't be free.
   But those people keep a-movin' and that's what tortures me.

4. Well, if they freed me from this prison, if that railroad train was mine,
   I bet I'd move it on a little farther down the line,
   Far from Folsom Prison, that's where I want to stay.
   And I'd let that lonesome whistle blow my blues away.

The Fightin' Side of Me

Words and Music by Merle Haggard

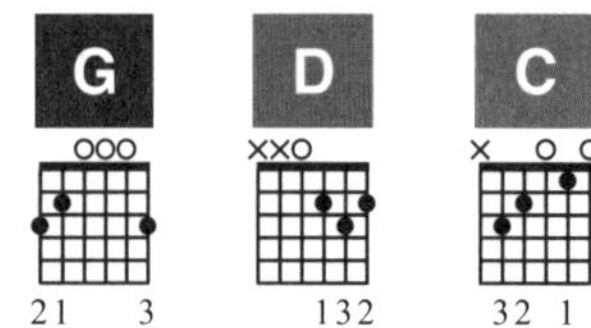

Verse
Moderate Country, in 2

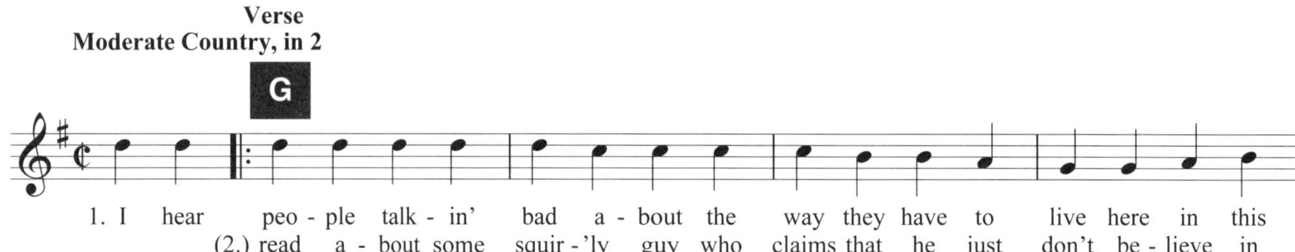

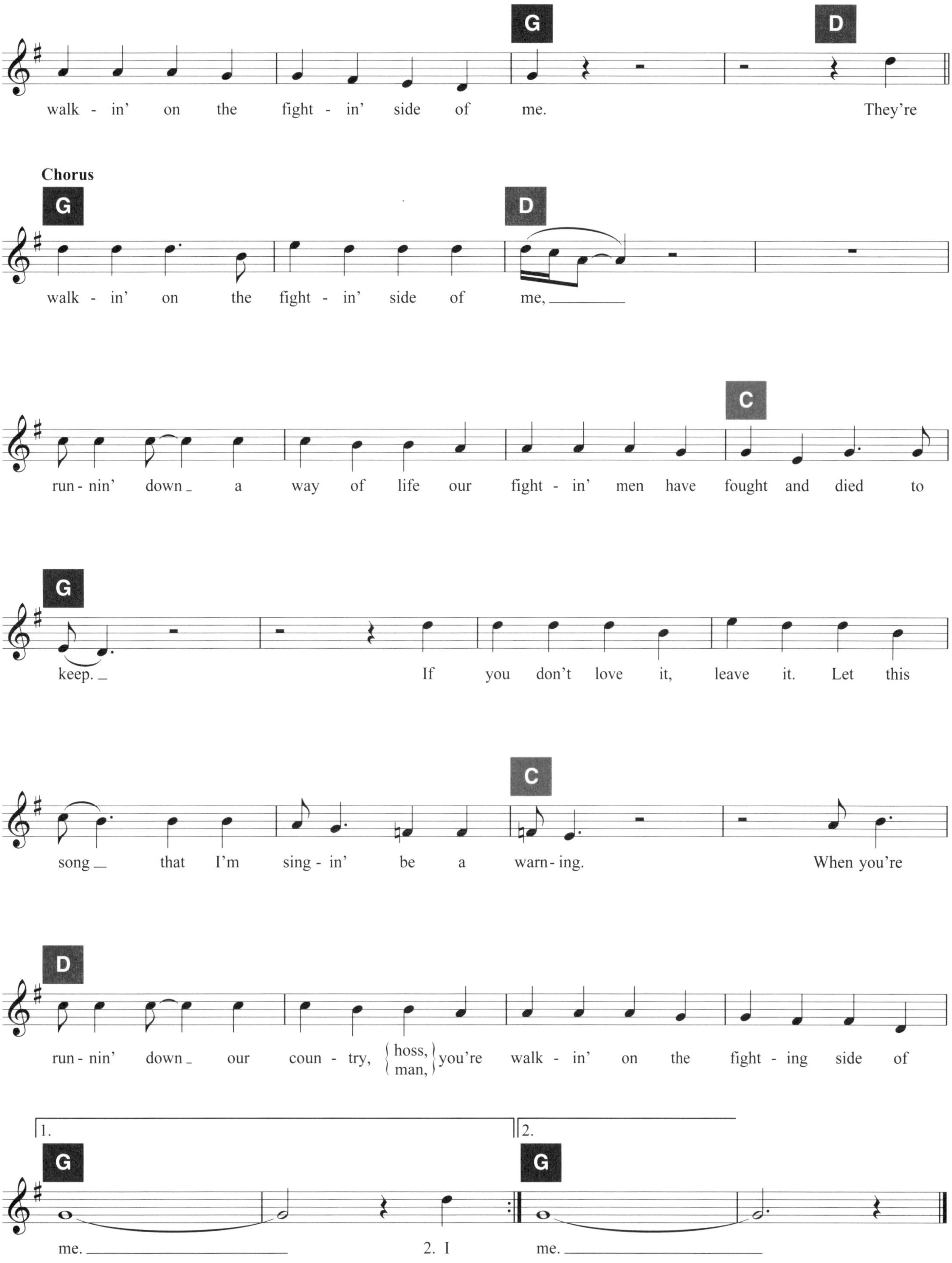

G D

walk - in' on the fight - in' side of me. They're

Chorus

G D

walk - in' on the fight - in' side of me,

C

run - nin' down a way of life our fight - in' men have fought and died to

G

keep. If you don't love it, leave it. Let this

C

song that I'm sing - in' be a warn - ing. When you're

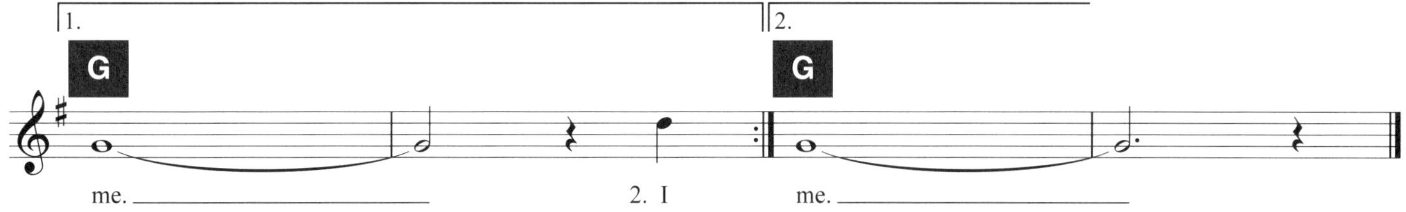

Garden Party

Words and Music by Rick Nelson

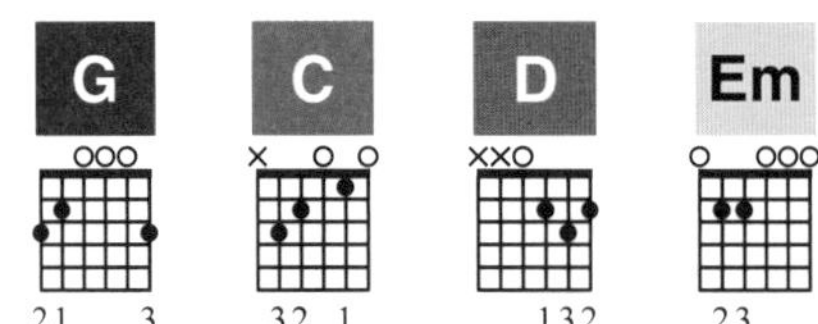

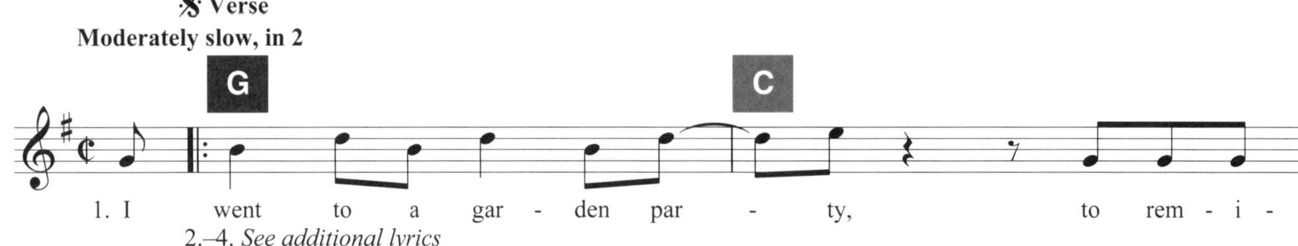

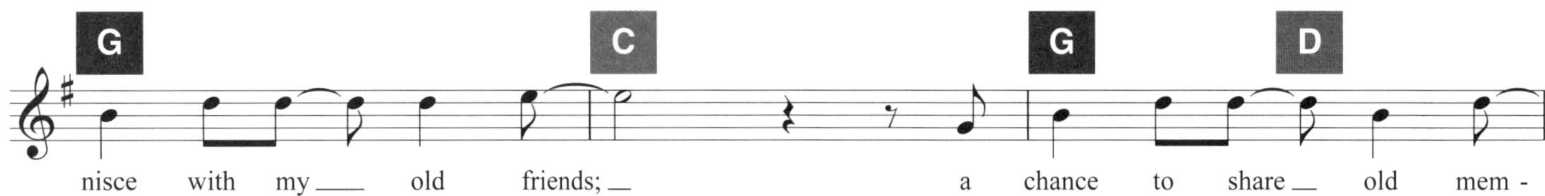

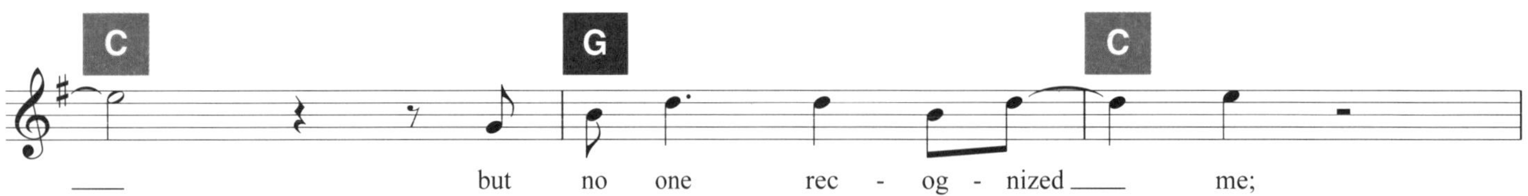

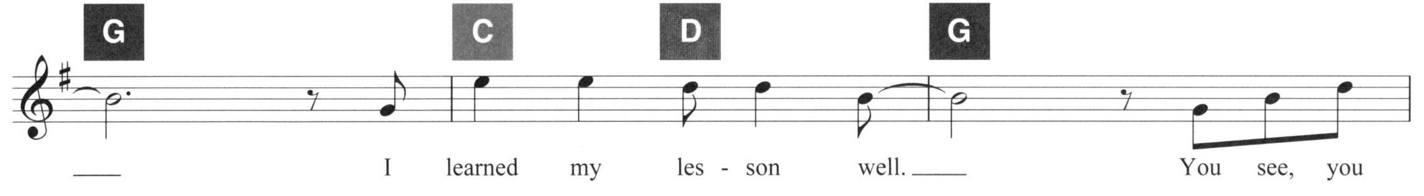

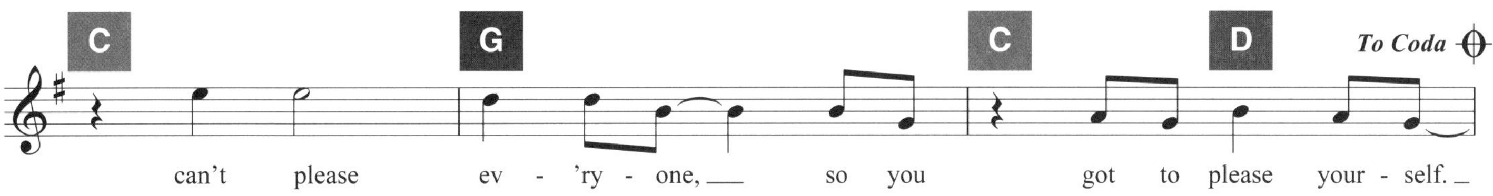

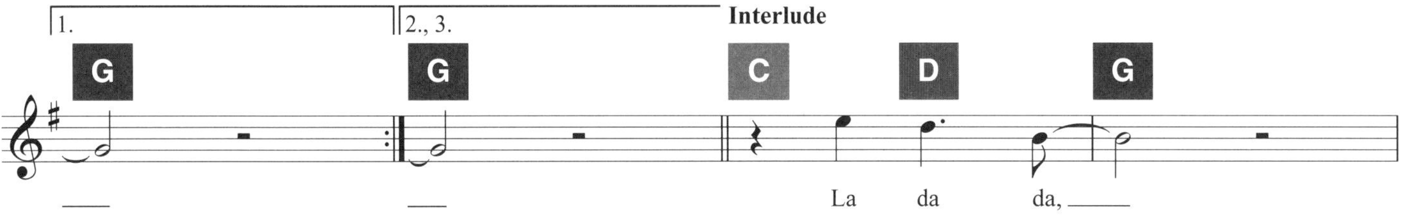

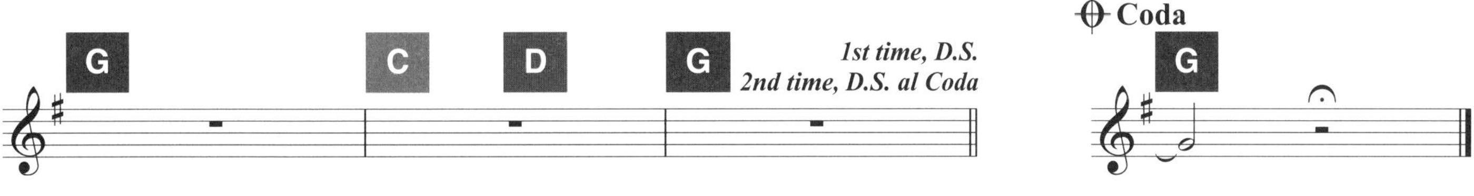

Additional Lyrics

2. People came for miles around; everyone was there.
   Yoko brought her walrus; there was magic in the air.
   And over in the corner, much to my surprise,
   Mr. Hughes hid in Dylan's shoes, wearing his disguise.

3. I played them all the old songs; I thought that's why they came.
   No one heard the music; we didn't look the same.
   I said hello to Mary Lou; she belongs to me.
   When I sang a song about a honky-tonk, it was time to leave.

4. Someone opened up a closet door and out stepped Johnny B. Goode,
   Playing guitar like a-ringin' a bell, and lookin' like he should.
   If you gotta play at garden parties, I wish you a lotta luck;
   But if memories were all I sang, I'd rather drive a truck.

Give Me That Old Time Religion

Traditional

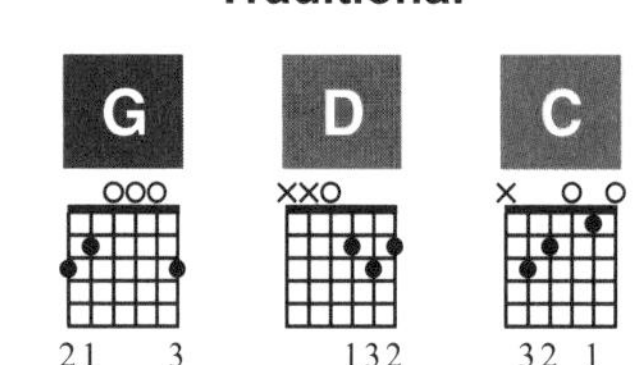

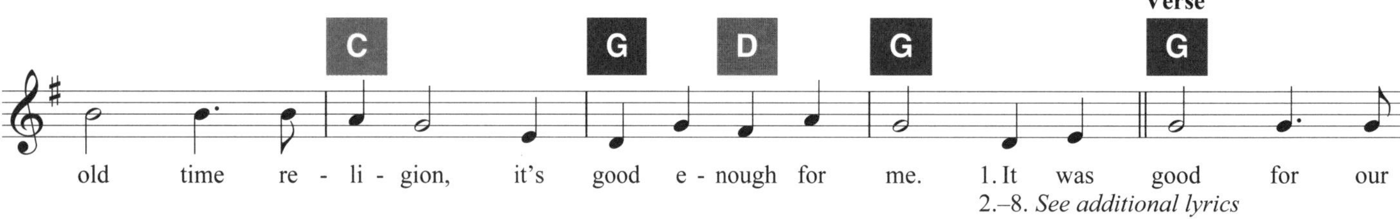

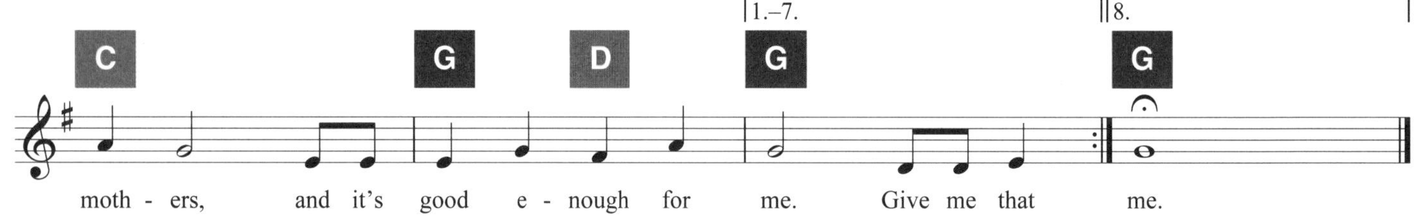

Additional Lyrics

2. Makes me love everybody,
   Makes me love everybody,
   Makes me love everybody,
   And it's good enough for me.

3. It has saved our fathers,
   It has saved our fathers,
   It has saved our fathers,
   And it's good enough for me.

4. It was good for the prophet Daniel,
   It was good for the prophet Daniel,
   It was good for the prophet Daniel,
   And it's good enough for me.

5. It was good for the Hebrew children,
   It was good for the Hebrew children,
   It was good for the Hebrew children,
   And it's good enough for me.

6. It was tried in the fiery furnace,
   It was tried in the fiery furnace,
   It was tried in the fiery furnace,
   And it's good enough for me.

7. It was good for Paul and Silas,
   It was good for Paul and Silas,
   It was good for Paul and Silas,
   And it's good enough for me.

8. It will do when I am dying,
   It will do when I am dying,
   It will do when I am dying,
   And it's good enough for me.

Have I Told You Lately That I Love You

Words and Music by Scott Wiseman

Green Green Grass of Home

Words and Music by Curly Putman

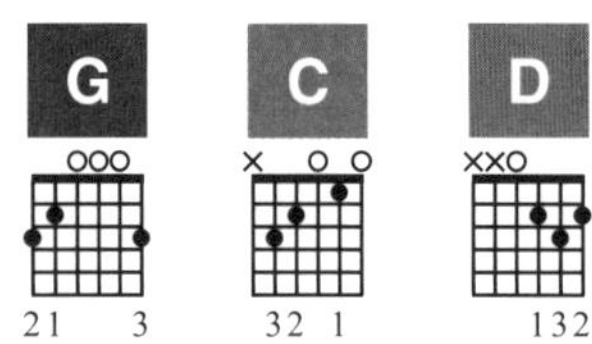

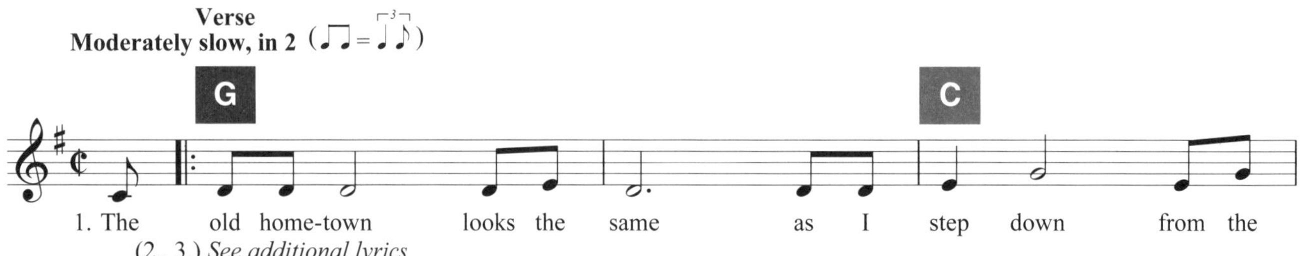

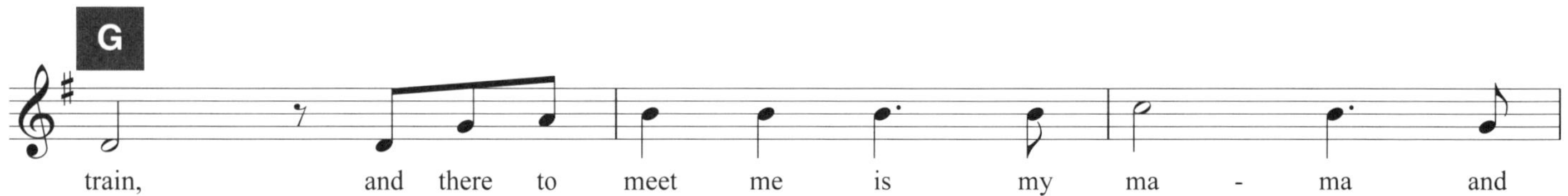

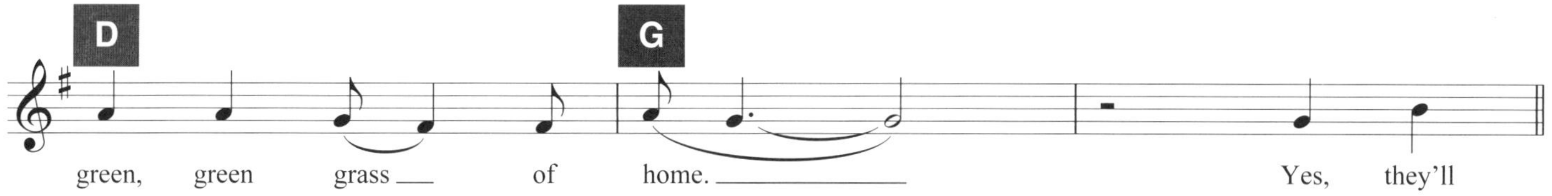

Additional Lyrics

2. The old house is still standing, though the paint is cracked and dry.
And there's that old oak tree that I used to play on.
Down the lane I walk with my sweet Mary, hair of gold and lips like cherries.
It's good to touch the green, green grass of home.

3. *(Spoken:) Then I awake, and look around me at four gray walls that surround me,*
And I realize that I was only dreaming.
For there's a guard and there's a sad, old padre. Arm in arm we'll walk at daybreak.
Again I'll touch the green, green grass of home.

He Stopped Loving Her Today

Words and Music by Bobby Braddock and Curly Putman

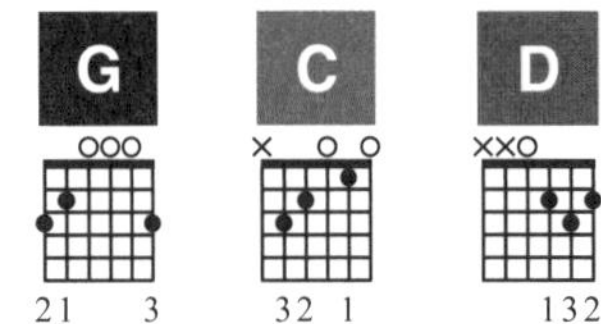

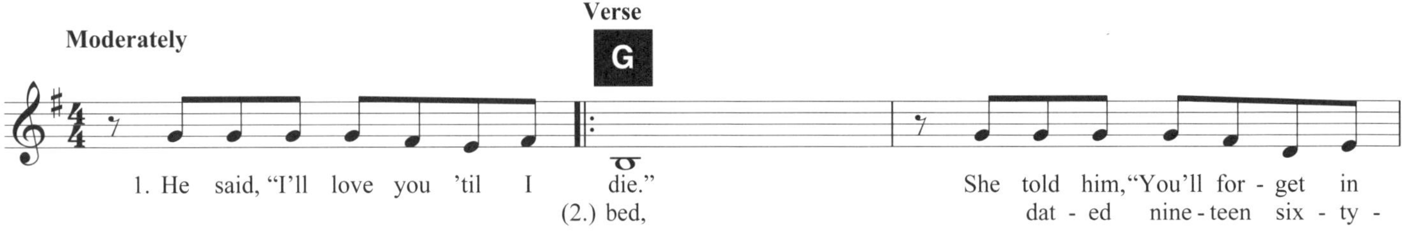

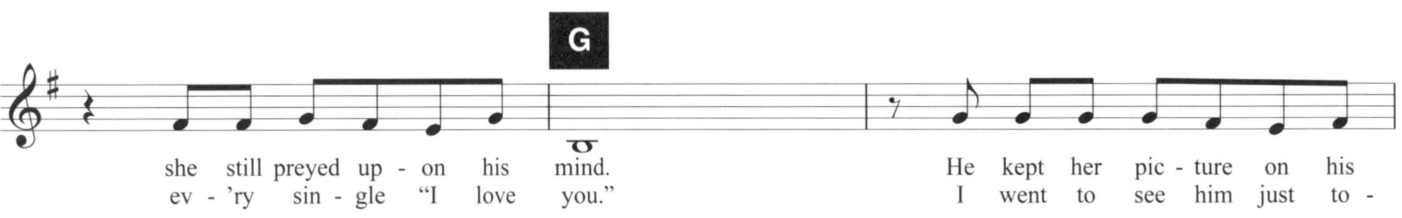

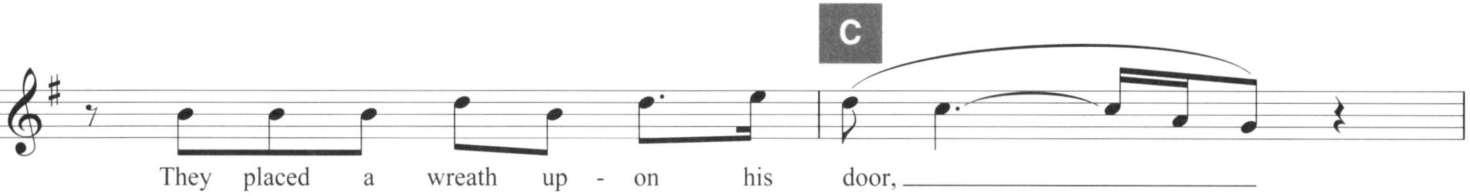

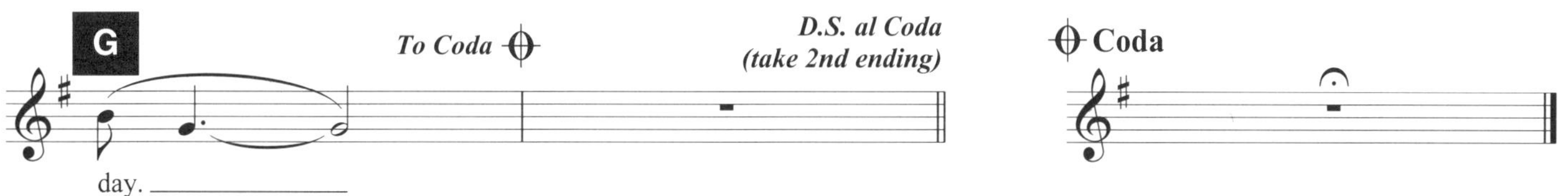

Additional Lyrics

3. *(Spoken:)* *You know, she came to see him one last time.*
We all wondered if she would.
And it came running through my mind:
This time he's over her for good.

He's Got the Whole World in His Hands

Home on the Range

Lyrics by Dr. Brewster Higley
Music by Dan Kelly

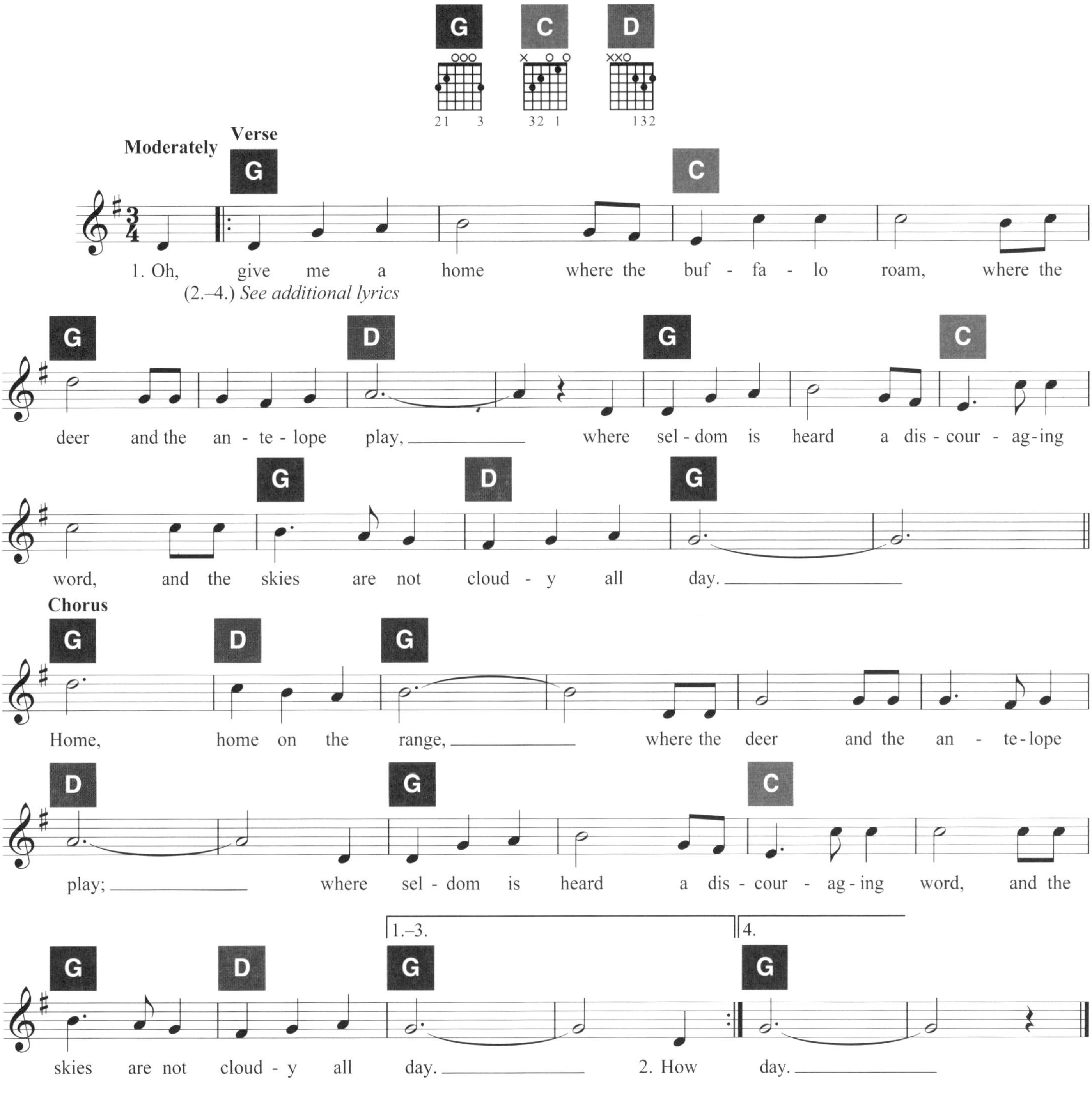

G C D

21 3 32 1 132

Moderately

Verse

G C
1. Oh, give me a home where the buf - fa - lo roam, where the
(2.–4.) *See additional lyrics*

G D G C
deer and the an - te - lope play, ___ where sel - dom is heard a dis - cour - ag - ing

G D G
word, and the skies are not cloud - y all day. ___

Chorus

G D G
Home, home on the range, ___ where the deer and the an - te - lope

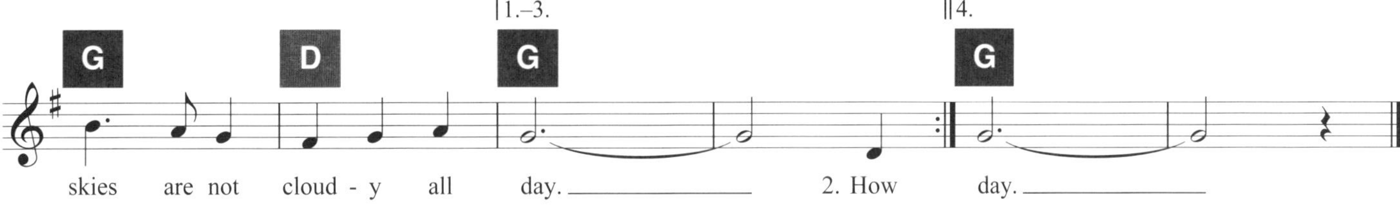

Additional Lyrics

2. How often at night, when the heavens are bright
From the light of the glittering stars,
Have I stood there amazed and asked as I gazed
If their glory exceeds that of ours.

3. Where the air is so pure and the zephyrs so free,
And the breezes so balmy and light;
Oh, I would not exchange my home on the range
For the glittering cities so bright.

4. Oh, give me a land where the bright diamond sand
Flows leisurely down with the stream,
Where the graceful white swan glides slowly along,
Like a maid in a heavenly dream.

Heartaches by the Number

Words and Music by Harlan Howard

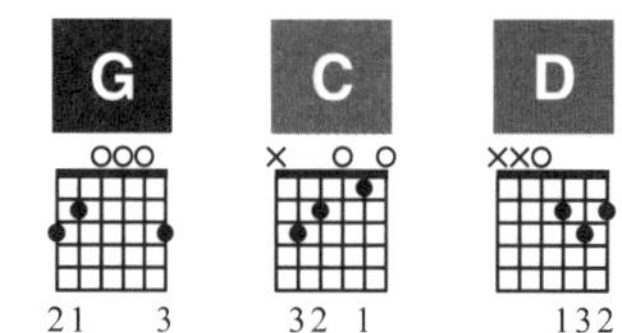

Verse

Moderately, in 2

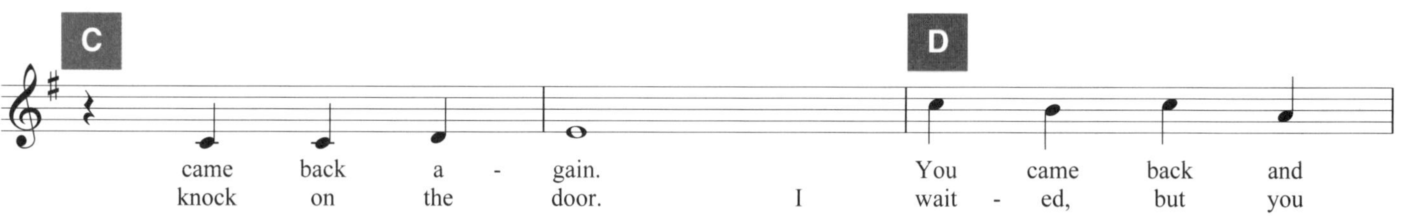

Chorus

G
C
heart - aches by the num - ber,
trou - bles by the

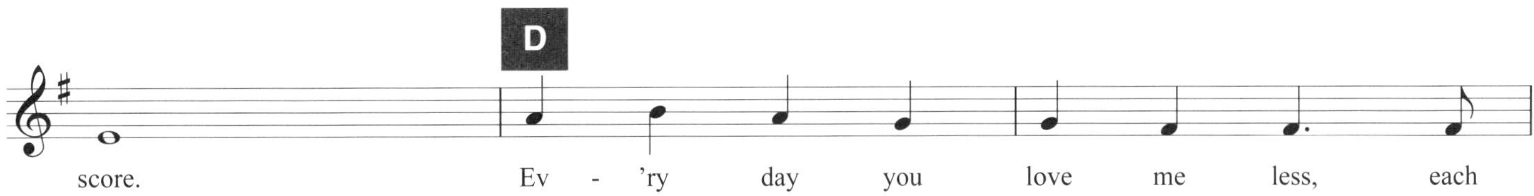
D
score.
Ev - 'ry day you love me less, each

G
day I love you more.
Yes, I've got

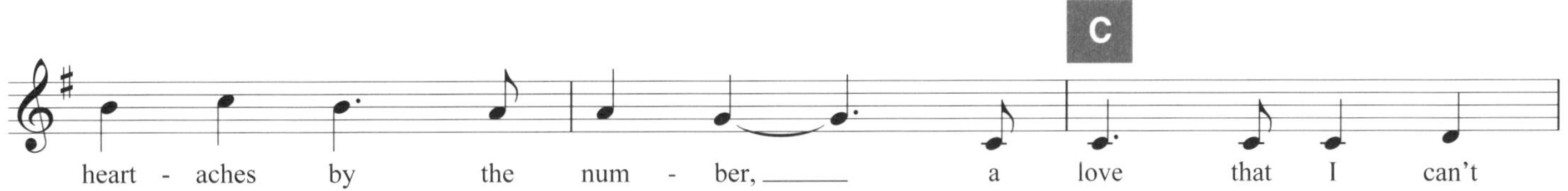
C
heart - aches by the num - ber,
a love that I can't

D
win;
but the day that I stop count - ing, that's the

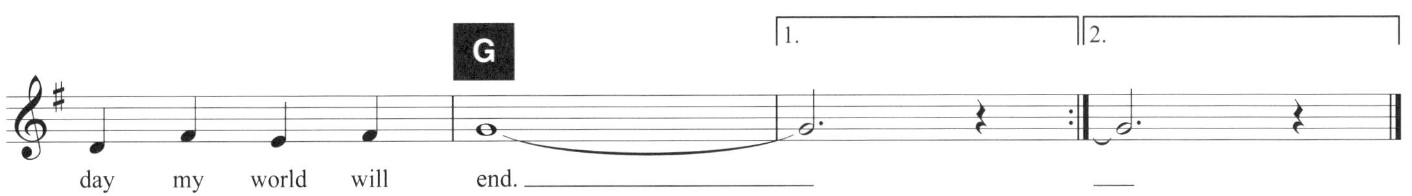
G
1.
2.
day my world will end.

Hound Dog

Words and Music by Jerry Leiber and Mike Stoller

I Fought the Law

Words and Music by Sonny Curtis

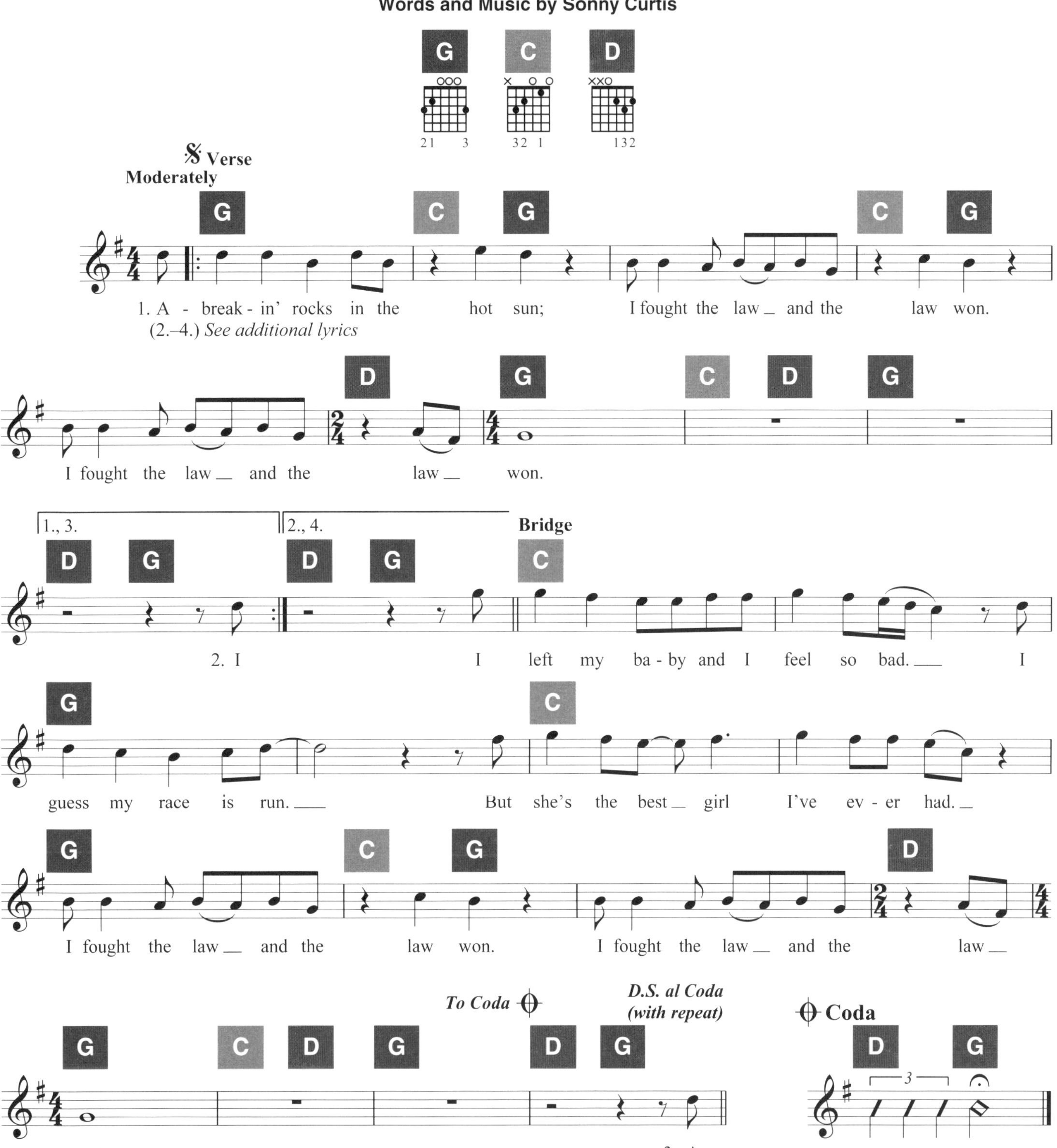

Additional Lyrics

2. I needed money 'cause I had none.
   I fought the law and the law won.
   I fought the law and the law won.

3. A-robbin' people with a six-gun.
   I fought the law and the law won.
   I fought the law and the law won.

4. I miss my baby and the good fun.
   I fought the law and the law won.
   I fought the law and the law won.

I Walk the Line

Words and Music by John R. Cash

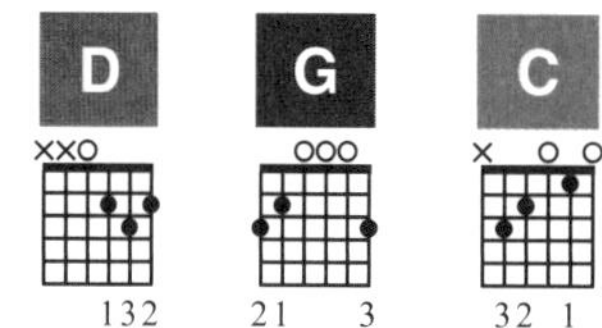

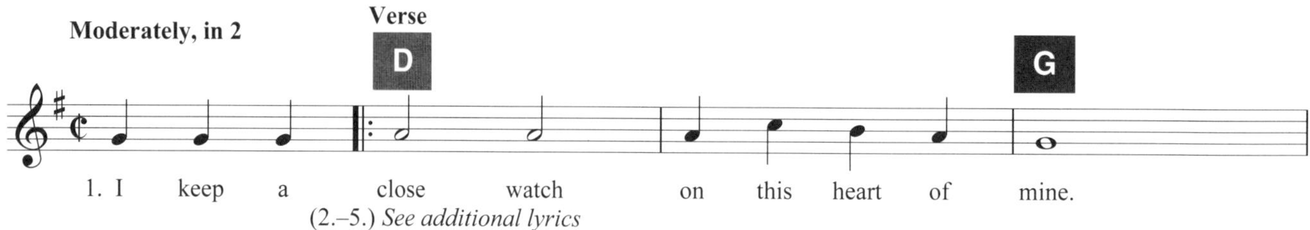

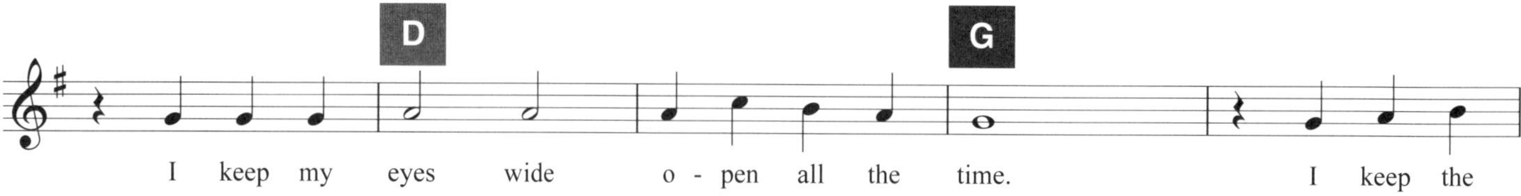

Additional Lyrics

2. I find it very easy to be true.
   I find myself alone when each day is through.
   Yes, I'll admit that I'm a fool for you.
   Because you're mine, I walk the line.

3. As sure as night is dark and day is light,
   I keep you on my mind both day and night.
   And happiness I've known proves that it's right.
   Because you're mine, I walk the line.

4. You've got a way to keep me on your side.
   You give me cause for love that I can't hide.
   For you I know I'd even try to turn the tide.
   Because you're mine, I walk the line.

5. I keep a close watch on this heart of mine.
   I keep my eyes wide open all the time.
   I keep the ends out for the tie that binds.
   Because you're mine, I walk the line.

I'm So Lonesome I Could Cry

Words and Music by Hank Williams

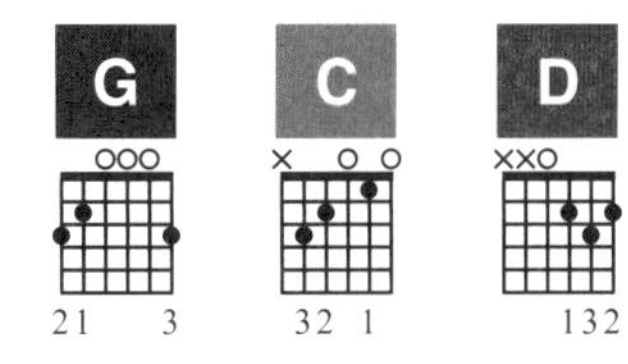

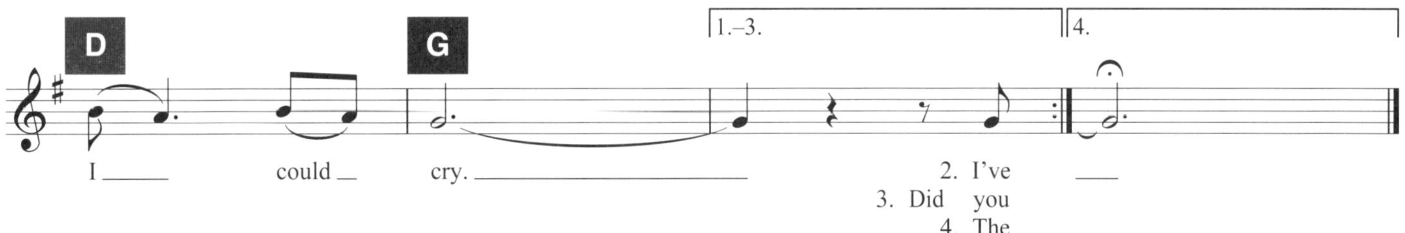

Additional Lyrics

2. I've never seen a night so long,
   When time goes crawling by.
   The moon just went behind a cloud
   To hide its face and cry.

3. Did you ever see a robin weep
   When leaves begin to die?
   That means he's lost the will to live.
   I'm so lonesome I could cry.

4. The silence of a falling star
   Lights up a purple sky.
   And as I wonder where you are,
   I'm so lonesome I could cry.

Jambalaya
(On the Bayou)

Words and Music by Hank Williams

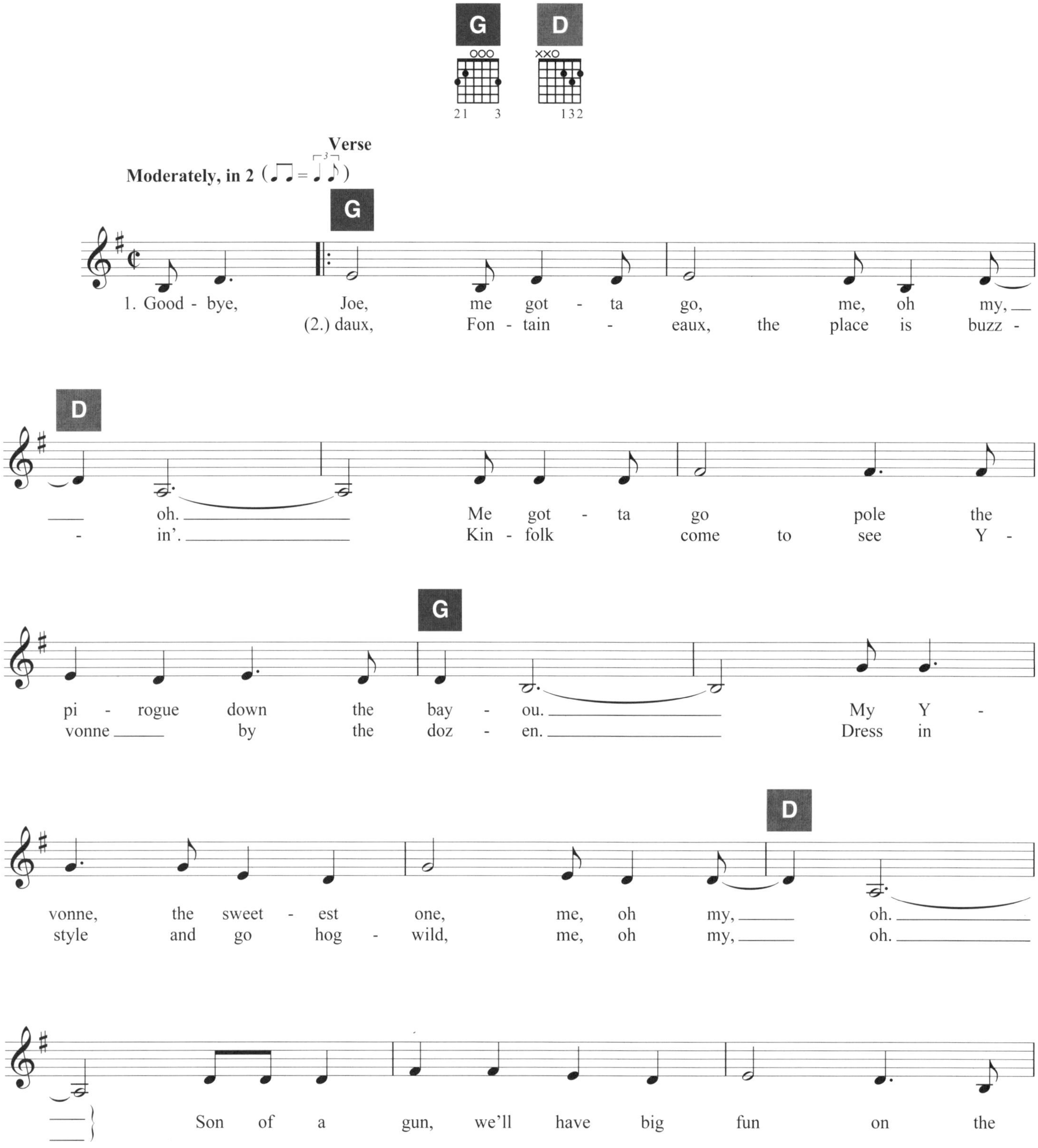

G D

21 3 132

Verse

Moderately, in 2

G

1. Good - bye, Joe, me got - ta go, me, oh my, —
(2.) daux, Fon - tain - eaux, the place is buzz -

D

— oh. —— Me got - ta go pole the
- in'. —— Kin - folk come to see Y -

G

pi - rogue down the bay - ou. —— My Y -
vonne —— by the doz - en. —— Dress in

D

vonne, the sweet - est one, me, oh my, —— oh. ——
style and go hog - wild, me, oh my, —— oh. ——

Chorus
G
G
bay - ou. Jam - ba - la - ya, and a craw - fish

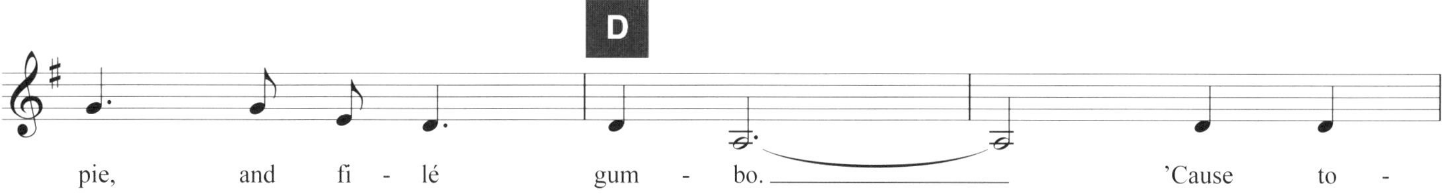
D
pie, and fi - lé gum - bo. 'Cause to -

G
night I'm gon - na see my ma cher a mi - o.

Pick gui - tar, fill fruit jar, and be

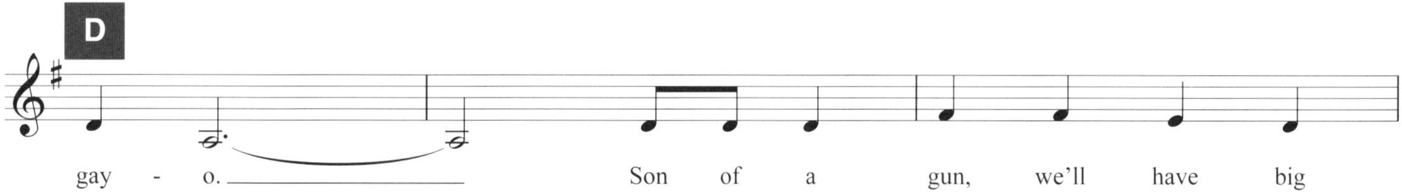
D
gay - o. Son of a gun, we'll have big

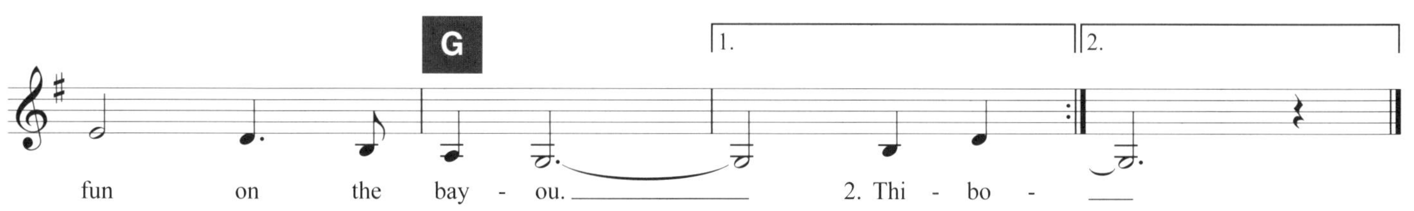
G
1.
2.
fun on the bay - ou. 2. Thi - bo -

Just a Closer Walk with Thee

Traditional
Arranged by Kenneth Morris

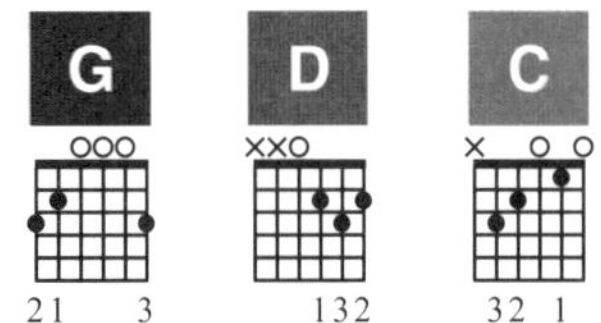

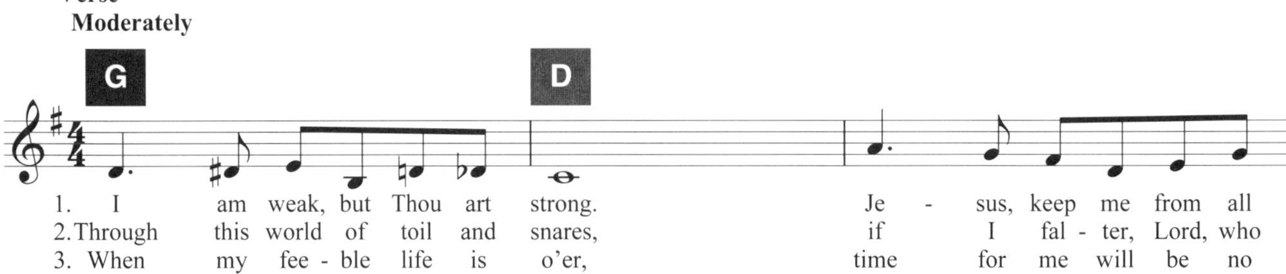

Keep on the Sunny Side

Words and Music by A.P. Carter

King of the Road

Words and Music by Roger Miller

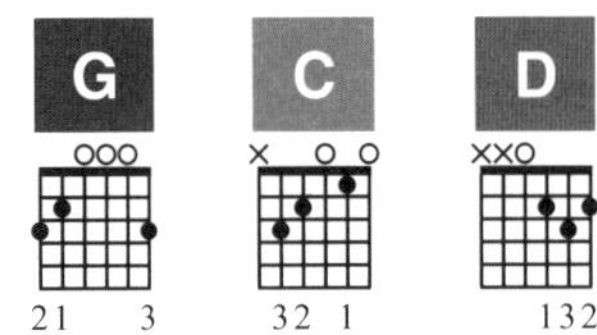

Verse
Moderate Shuffle

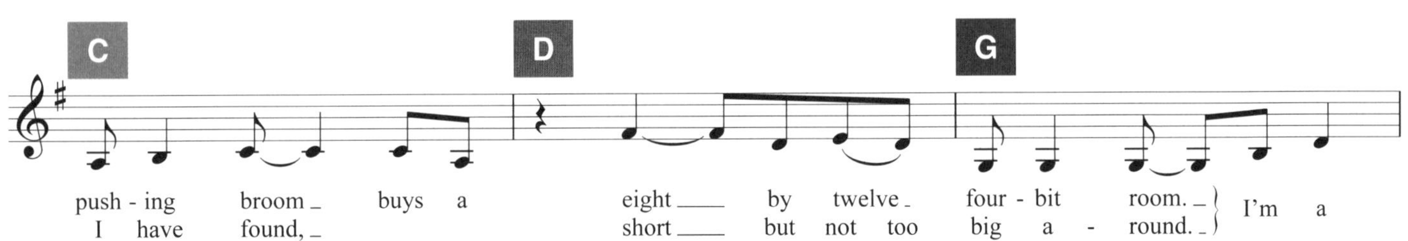

C
D
N.C.
To Coda
man of means by no means, king of the road.

1.
2.
Bridge
G
G
G
I know ev - er - y en - gi - neer on

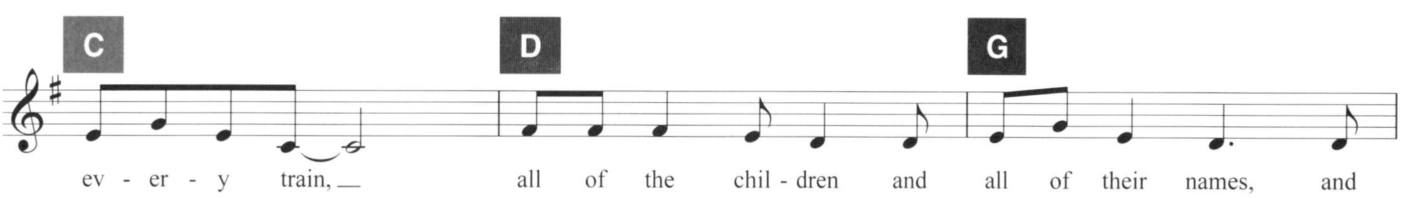
C
D
G
ev - er - y train, all of the chil - dren and all of their names, and

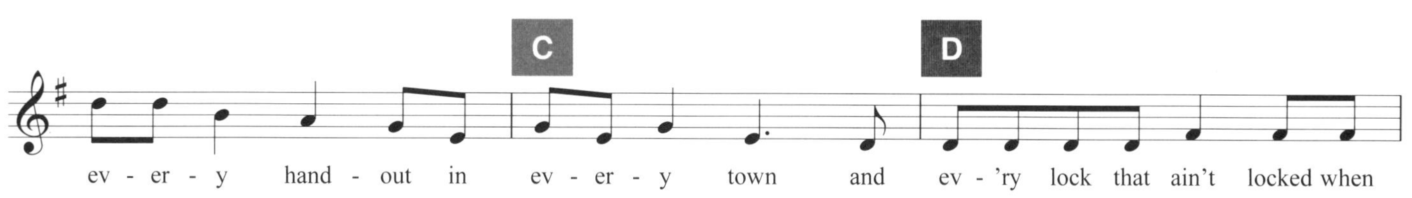
C
D
ev - er - y hand - out in ev - er - y town and ev - 'ry lock that ain't locked when

D.C. al Coda
(Lyric 1)
Coda
G
no one's a - round. I sing:

Kiss an Angel Good Mornin'

Words and Music by Ben Peters

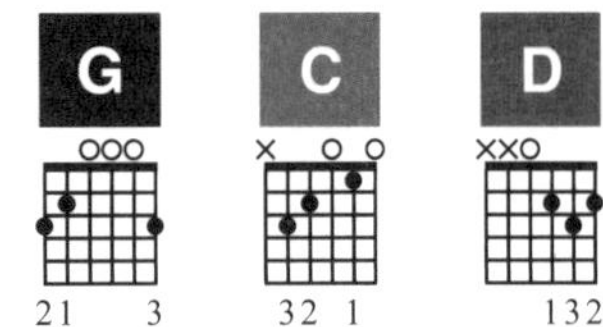

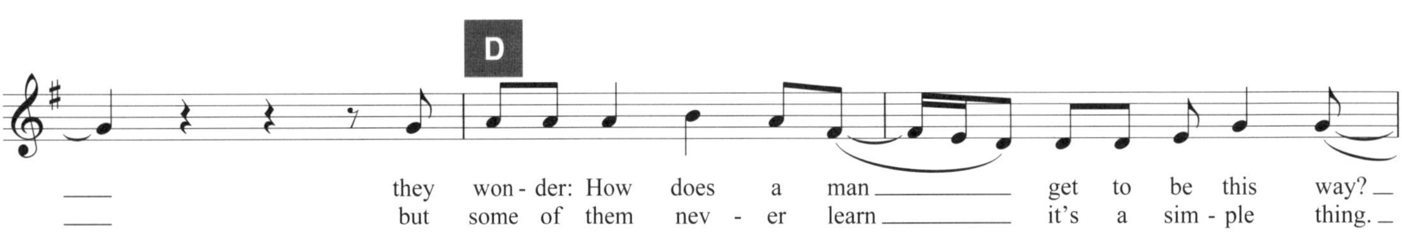

D
G
ev - 'ry time they ask me why, I just smile and say:
an - swer is in this song that I al - ways sing:

Chorus
G
D
You've got to kiss an an - gel good morn - in'
Kiss an an - gel good morn - in'
and

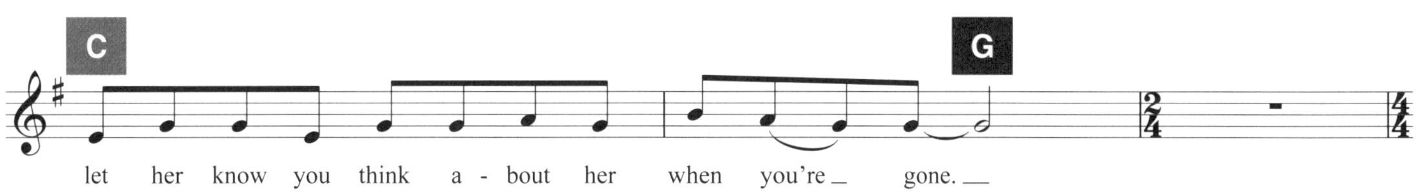
C
G
let her know you think a - bout her when you're gone.

D
C
To Coda
Kiss an an - gel good morn - in' and love her like the dev - il when you

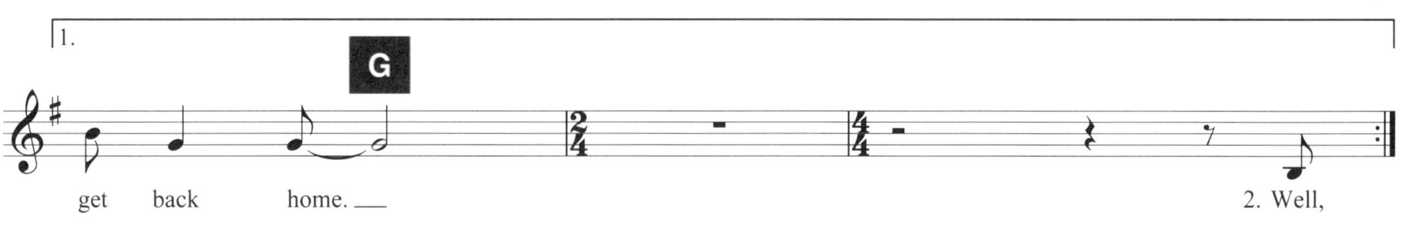
1.
G
get back home.
2. Well,

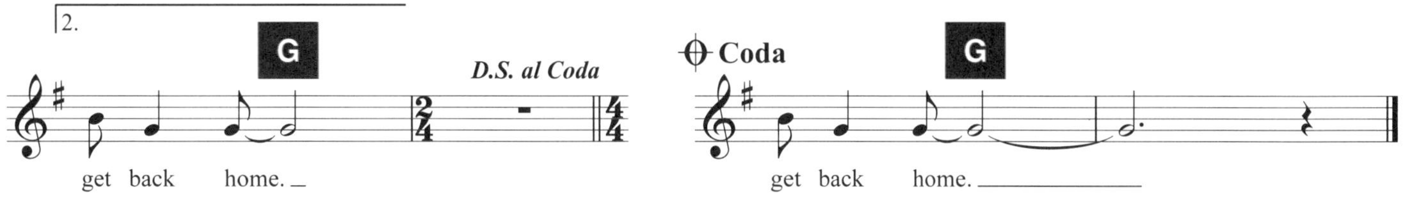
2.
G
D.S. al Coda
get back home.
Coda
G
get back home.

Kum Ba Yah

Traditional Spiritual

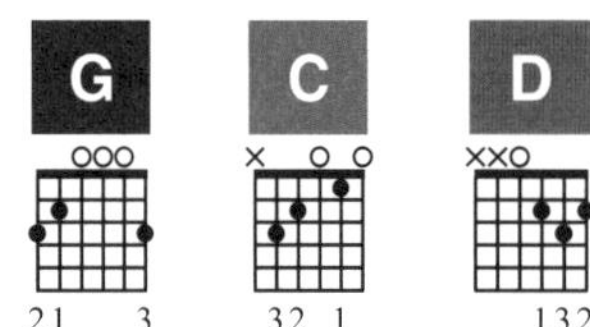

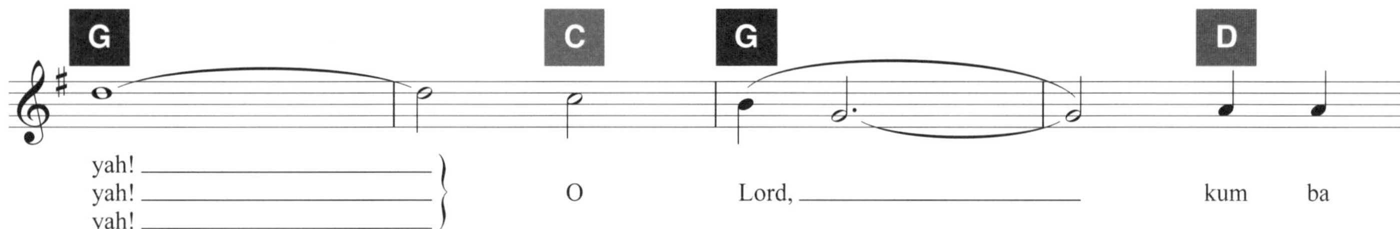

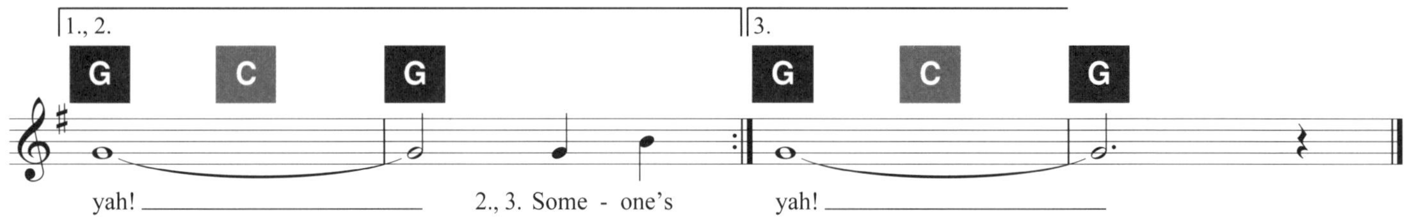

Make the World Go Away

Words and Music by Hank Cochran

La Bamba

By Ritchie Valens

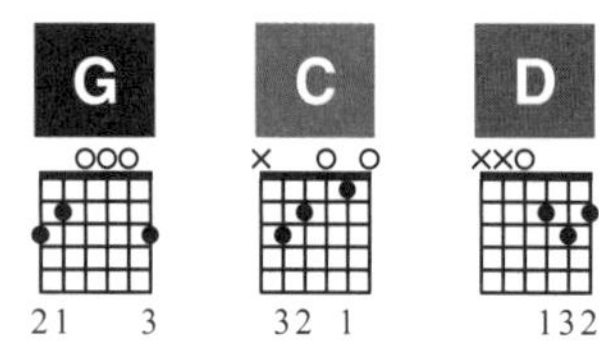

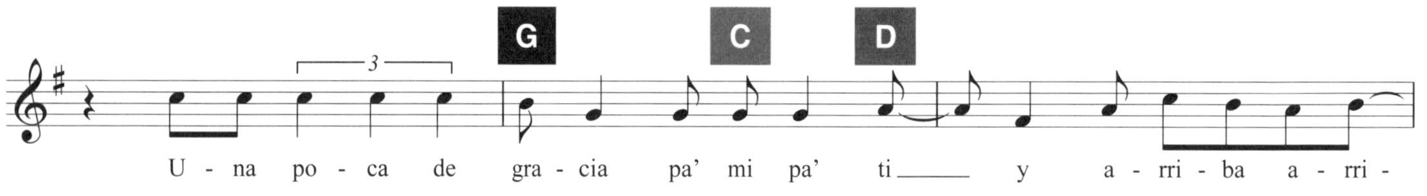

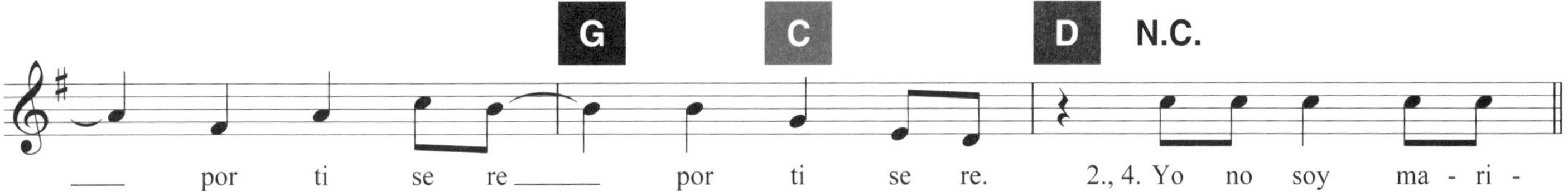
G
C
D
N.C.
__ por ti se re __ por ti se re. 2., 4. Yo no soy ma - ri -

Verse
G
C
D
G
C
D
ne - ro. Yo no soy ma - ri - ne - ro, soy ca - pi - tan, _

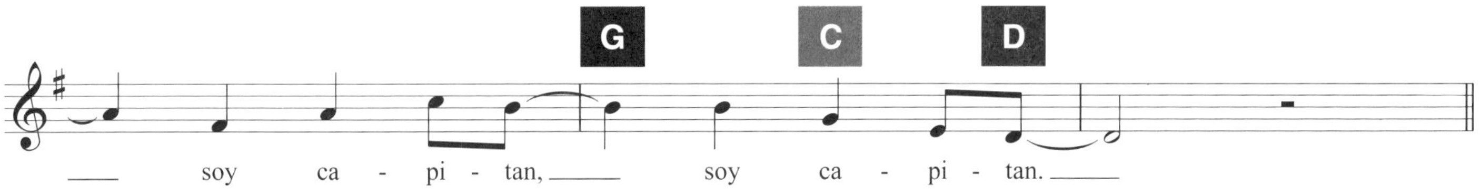
G
C
D
__ soy ca - pi - tan, __ soy ca - pi - tan. __

Chorus
G
C
D
G
C
D
Bam - ba __ bam - ba. Bam - ba __ bam -

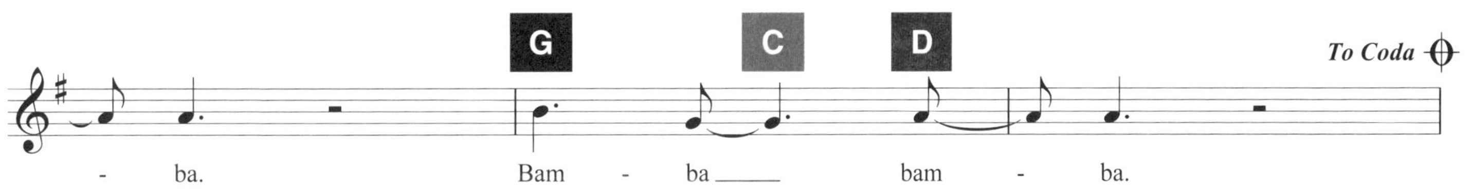
G
C
D
To Coda
- ba. Bam - ba __ bam - ba.

G
C
D
N.C.
D.S. al Coda
Coda
G
Bam - ba __ bam... __ 3. Pa - ra bai - lar la bam -

Last Kiss

Words and Music by Wayne Cochran

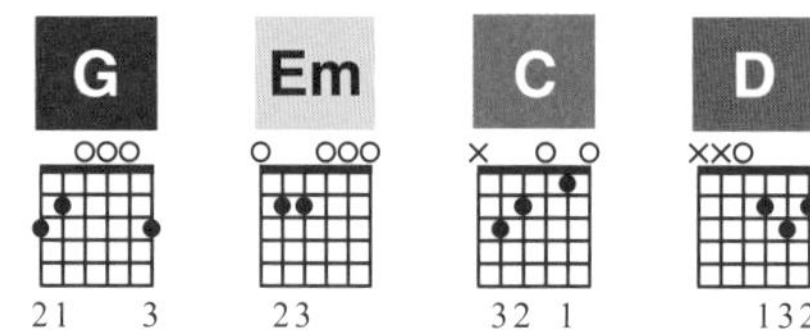

Intro-Chorus

Moderately fast

G Em C

Well, where, oh, where can my ba - by be? The Lord took her a -

D G Em

way from me. She's gone to heav - en, so I got to be good so

C D G

I can see my ba - by when I leave this world.

N.C.

Verse

G Em

1. We were out on a date in my dad - dy's car;
2. Well, when I woke up, the rain was pour - ing down;

C D G

we had - n't driv - en ver - y far. There in the road
there were peo - ple stand - in' all a - round. Some - thing warm a - run - nin'

Em C D

straight a - head, a car was stalled; the en - gine was dead.
in my eyes, but I found my ba - by some - how that night. I

G Em C
I could-n't stop, so I swerved to the right. I'll nev - er for - get the
raised her head and then she smiled and said, "Hold me, dar - ling, for a
D G Em
sound that night: the cry - in' tires, the bust - in' glass, the
lit - tle while." I held her close, I kissed her our last kiss. I
1.
C D G N.C.
pain - ful scream that I heard last. Well,
found a love that I
2.
D G Em
knew I would miss. But now she's gone; e - ven though I hold her tight, I
C D G N.C.
lost my love, my life that night. Well,
Outro-Chorus
G Em C
where, oh, where can my ba - by be? The Lord took her a -
D G Em
way from me. She's gone to heav - en, so I got to be good so
C D G
I can see my ba - by when I leave this world.

Let It Be

Words and Music by John Lennon and Paul McCartney

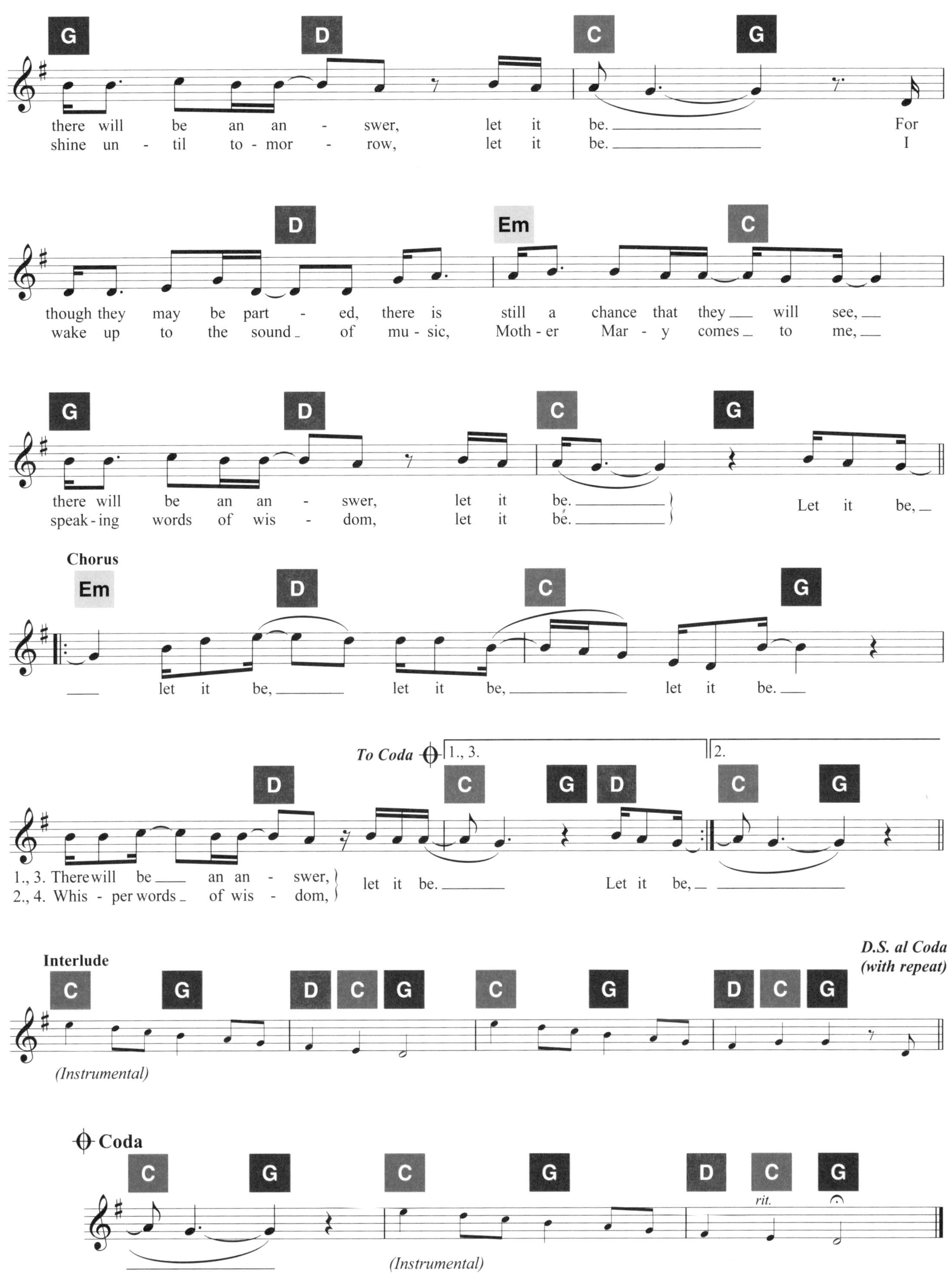
G
D
C
G
there will be an an - swer, let it be. For
shine un - til to - mor - row, let it be. I
D
Em
C
though they may be part - ed, there is still a chance that they will see,
wake up to the sound of mu - sic, Moth - er Mar - y comes to me,
G
D
C
G
there will be an an - swer, let it be.
speak - ing words of wis - dom, let it be.
Let it be,
Chorus
Em
D
C
G
let it be, let it be, let it be.
To Coda
1., 3.
2.
D
C
G
D
C
G
1., 3. There will be an an - swer,
2., 4. Whis - per words of wis - dom,
let it be.
Let it be,
Interlude
C
G
D
C
G
C
G
D
C
G
D.S. al Coda
(with repeat)
(Instrumental)
Coda
C
G
C
G
D
C
G
rit.
(Instrumental)

Mama Tried

Words and Music by Merle Haggard

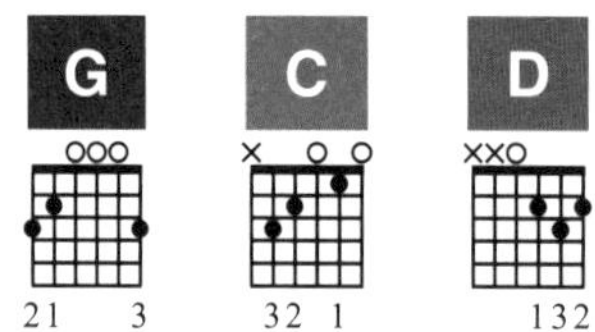

Intro
Moderately

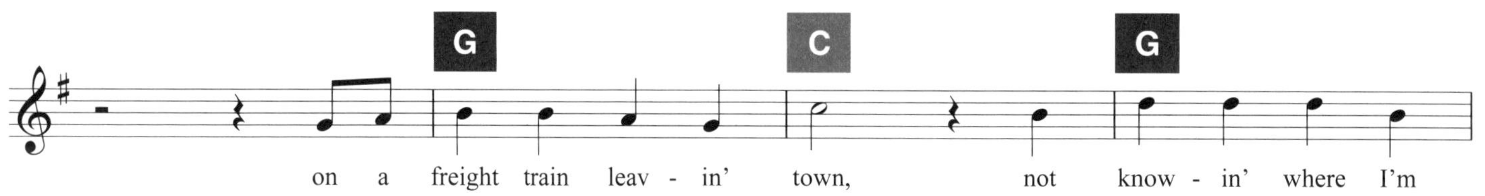

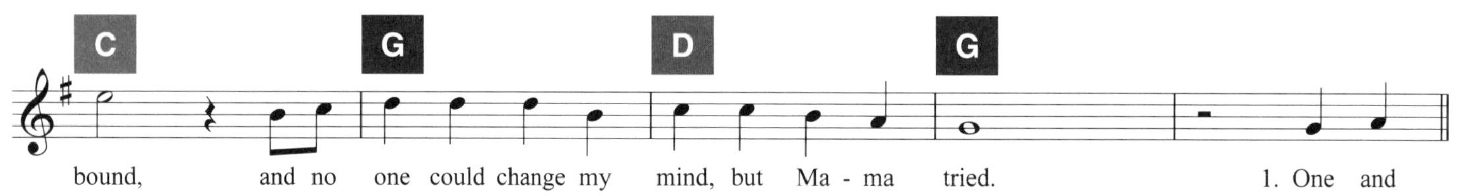

Verse

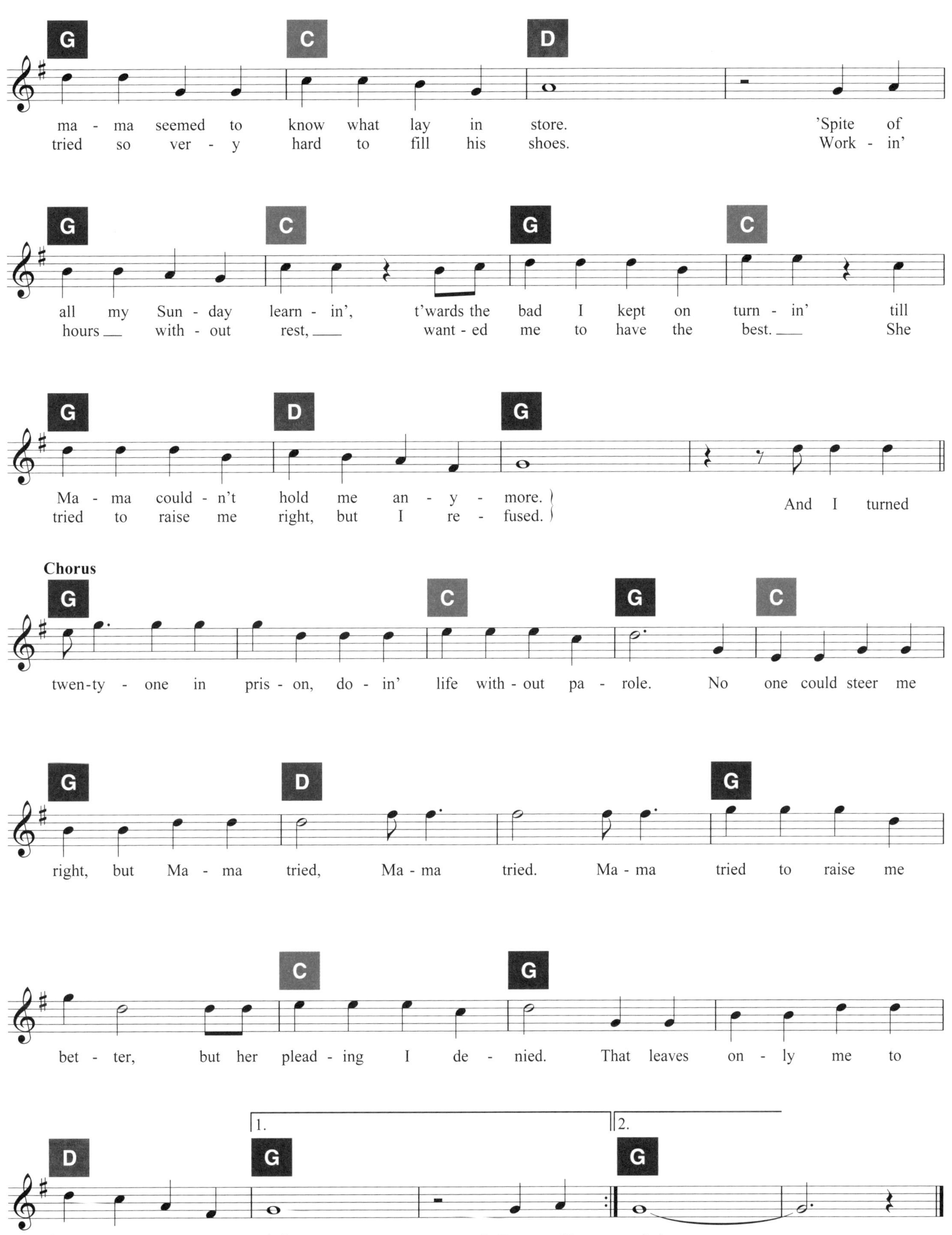
G C D
ma - ma seemed to know what lay in store. 'Spite of
tried so ver - y hard to fill his shoes. Work - in'
G C G C
all my Sun - day learn - in', t'wards the bad I kept on turn - in' till
hours with - out rest, want - ed me to have the best. She
G D G
Ma - ma could - n't hold me an - y - more.
tried to raise me right, but I re - fused.
And I turned
Chorus
G C G C
twen-ty - one in pris - on, do - in' life with - out pa - role. No one could steer me
G D G
right, but Ma - ma tried, Ma - ma tried. Ma - ma tried to raise me
C G
bet - ter, but her plead - ing I de - nied. That leaves on - ly me to
1. 2.
D G G
blame, 'cause Ma - ma tried. 2. Dear ol' tried.

Mammas Don't Let Your Babies Grow Up to Be Cowboys

Words and Music by Ed Bruce and Patsy Bruce

G
C
D
21 3
32 1
132

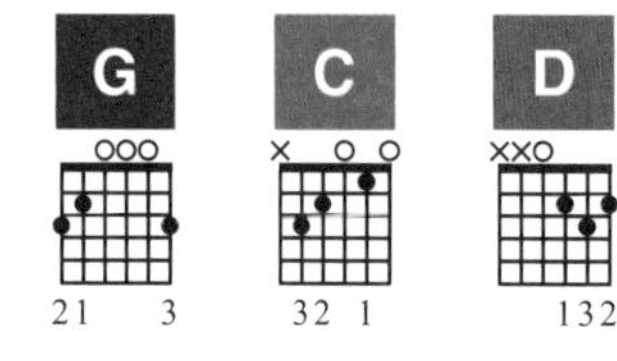

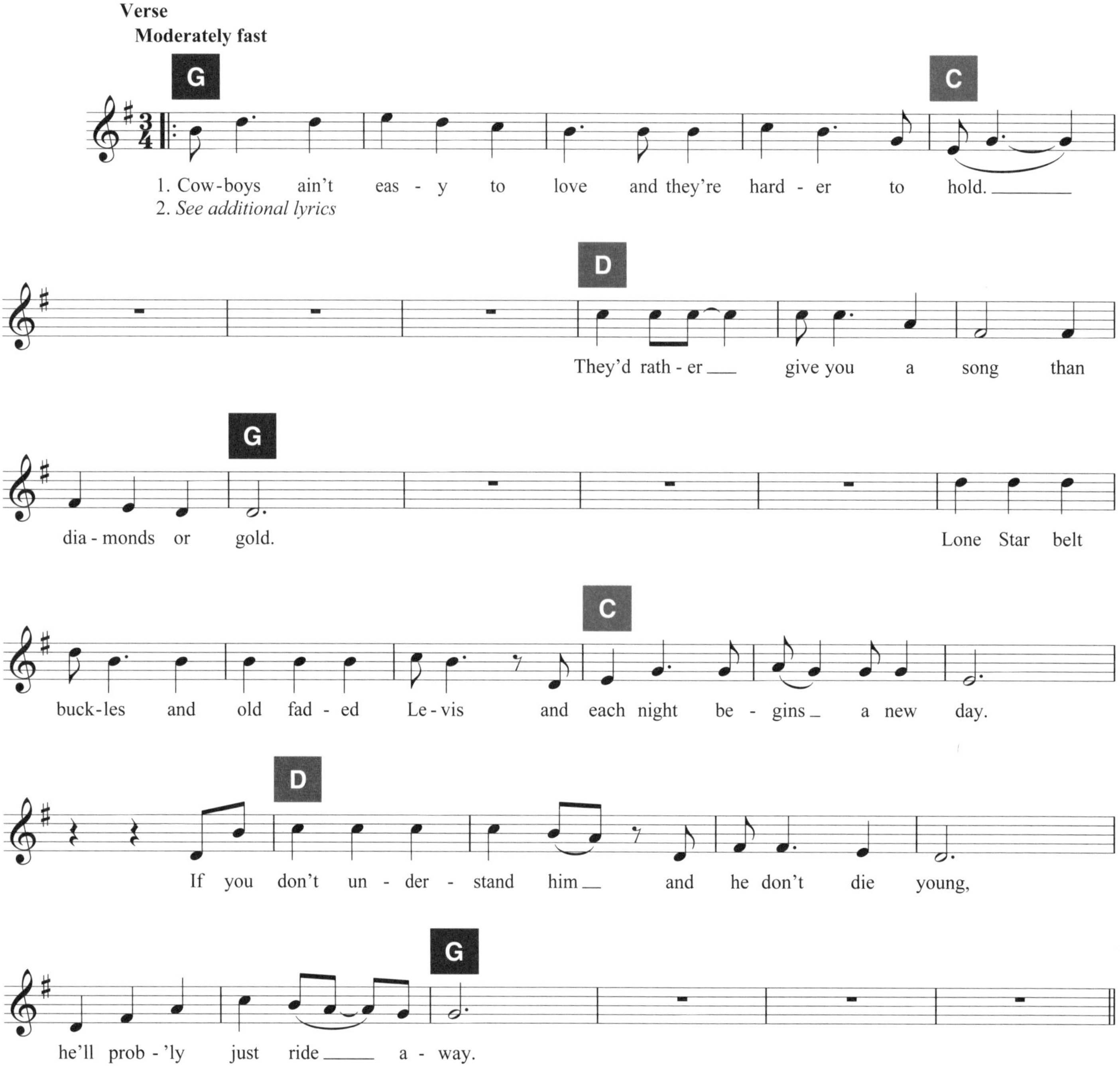

Verse
Moderately fast
G
C
1. Cow-boys ain't eas - y to love and they're hard - er to hold.
2. *See additional lyrics*
D
They'd rath - er give you a song than
G
dia - monds or gold.
Lone Star belt
C
buck-les and old fad - ed Le - vis and each night be - gins a new day.
D
If you don't un - der - stand him and he don't die young,
G
he'll prob - 'ly just ride a - way.

Additional Lyrics

2. Cowboys like smoky old poolrooms and clear mountain mornings,
Little warm puppies and children, and girls of the night.
Them that don't know him won't like him,
And them that do sometimes won't know how to take him,
He ain't wrong, he's just different,
But his pride won't let him do things to make you think he's right.

Oh! Susanna

Words and Music by Stephen C. Foster

Additional Lyrics

2. It rained all night the day I left,
 The weather it was dry.
 The sun so hot I froze to death,
 Susanna, don't you cry.

3. I had a dream the other night
 When everything was still.
 I thought I saw Susanna
 A-coming down the hill.

4. The buckwheat cake was in her mouth,
 The tear was in her eye.
 Say I, "I'm coming from the South,
 Susanna, don't you cry."

Pick Me Up on Your Way Down

Words and Music by Harlan Howard

Okie from Muskogee

Words and Music by Merle Haggard and Roy Edward Burris

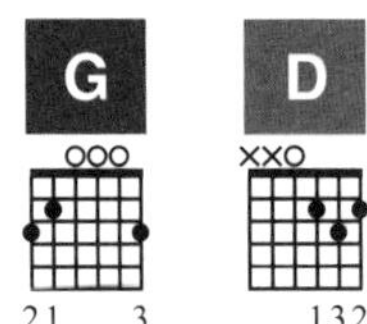

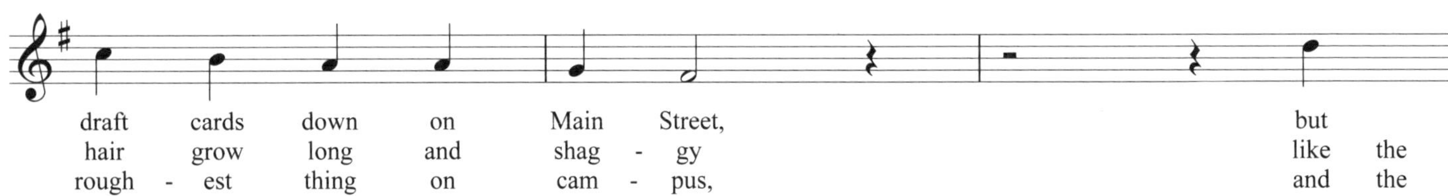

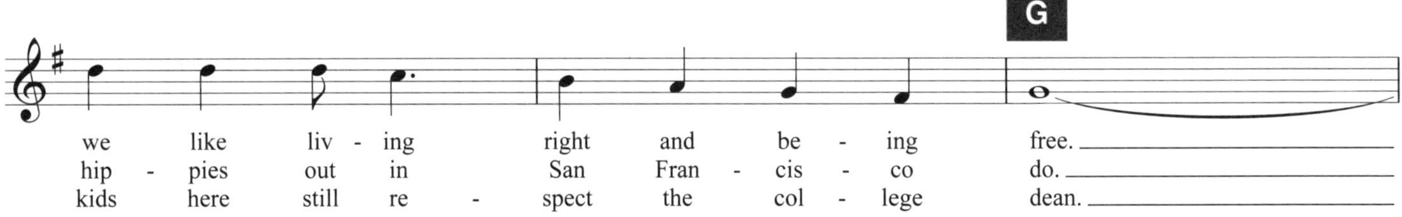

Chorus
G
And I'm proud to be an O - kie from Mus -

ko - gee; a place where e - ven

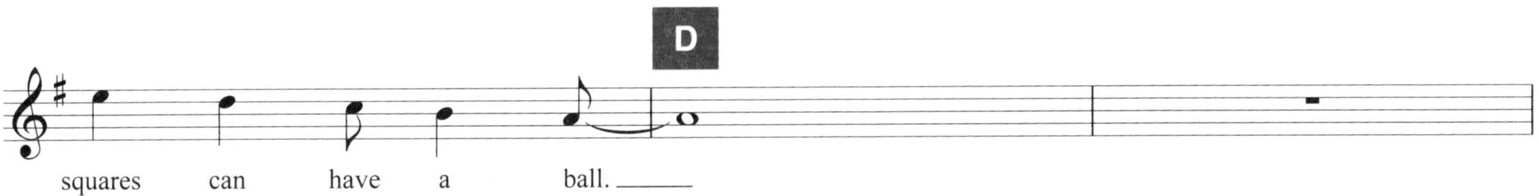
D
squares can have a ball.

We still wave Ol' Glo - ry down at the court - house.

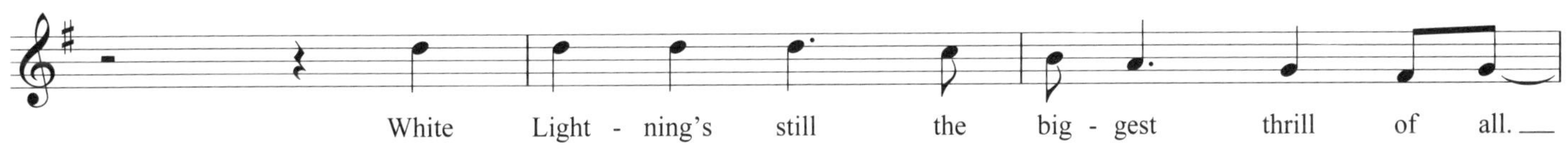
White Light - ning's still the big - gest thrill of all.

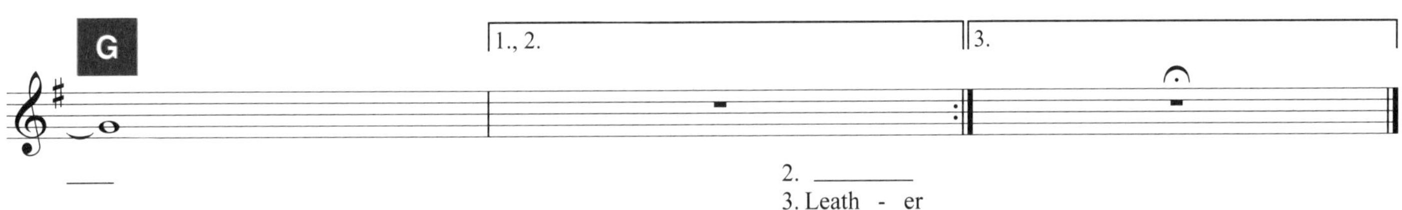
G
1., 2.
3.
2.
3. Leath - er

Proud Mary

Words and Music by John Fogerty

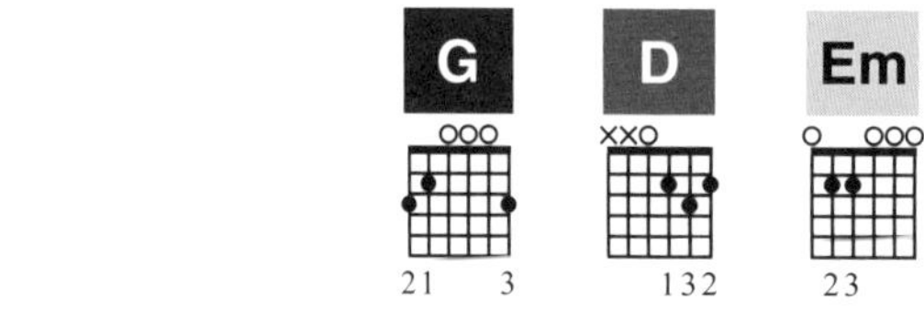

Verse

Moderate Rock

G

1. Left a good job ___ in the cit - y, work - in' for the man ev - 'ry

2., 3. *See additional lyrics*

Additional Lyrics

2. Cleaned a lot of plates in Memphis,
   Pumped a lot of 'pane in New Orleans,
   But I never saw the good side of the city,
   Until I hitched a ride on a river boat queen.

3. If you come down to the river,
   Bet you gonna find some people who live.
   You don't have to worry 'cause you have no money.
   People on the river are happy to give.

Rock of Ages

Words by August M. Toplady
v. 1, 2, 4 altered by Thomas Cotterill
Music by Thomas Hastings

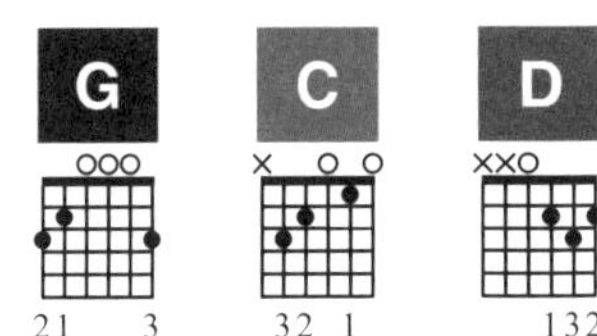

Verse
Moderately

Additional Lyrics

2. Could my tears forever flow,
   Could my zeal no languor know,
   These for sin could not atone;
   Thou must save, and Thou alone.
   In my hand no price I bring;
   Simply to Thy cross I cling.

3. Nothing in my hand I bring;
   Simply to Thy cross I cling.
   Naked, come to Thee for dress;
   Helpless, look to Thee for grace.
   Foul, I to the fountain fly;
   Wash me, Savior, or I die.

4. While I draw this fleeting breath,
   When my eyes shall close in death,
   When I rise to worlds unknown
   And behold Thee on Thy throne,
   Rock of Ages, cleft for me,
   Let me hide myself in Thee.

Ring of Fire

Words and Music by Merle Kilgore and June Carter

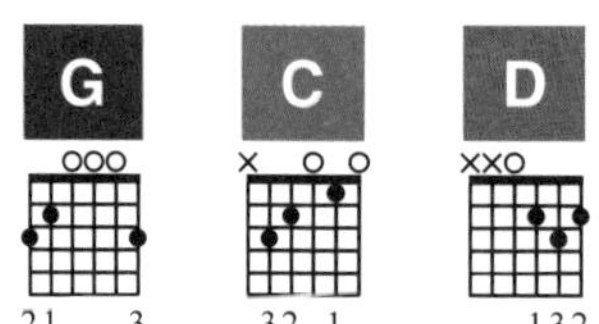

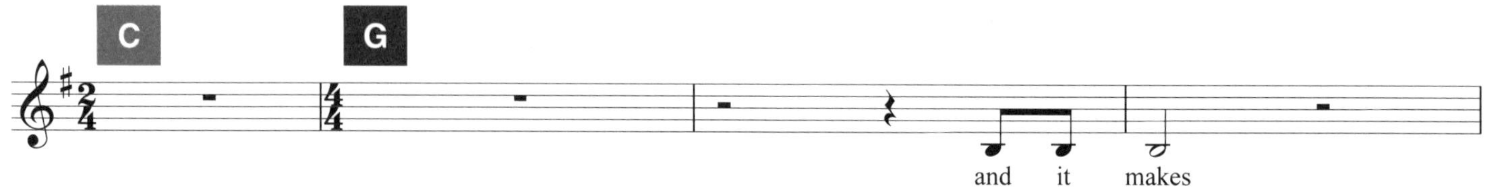

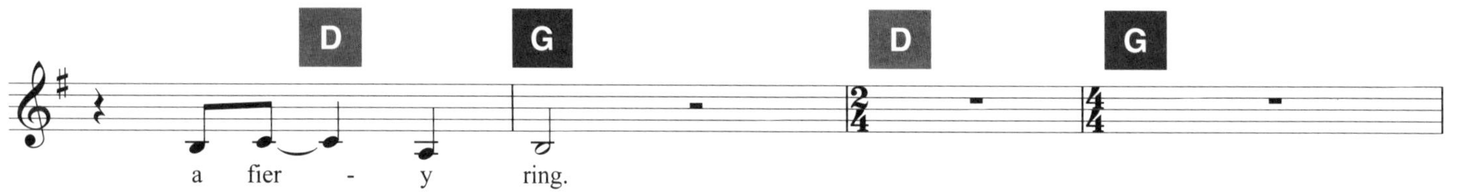

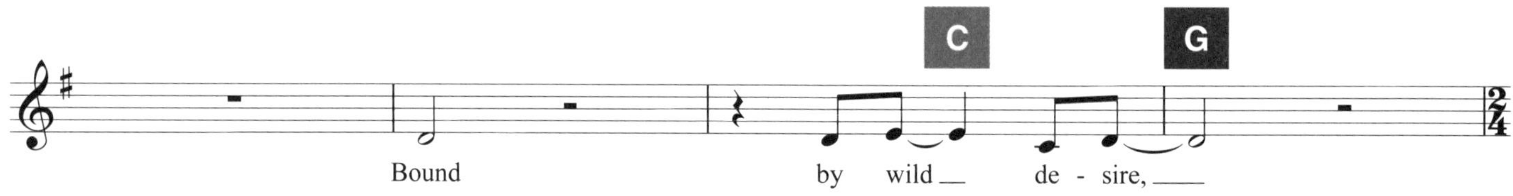

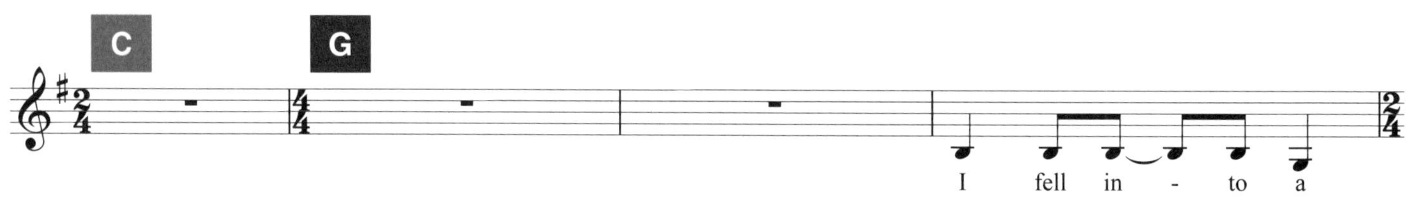

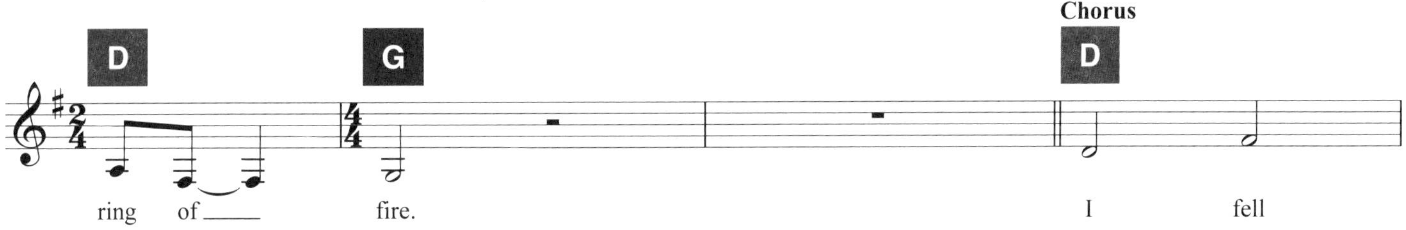

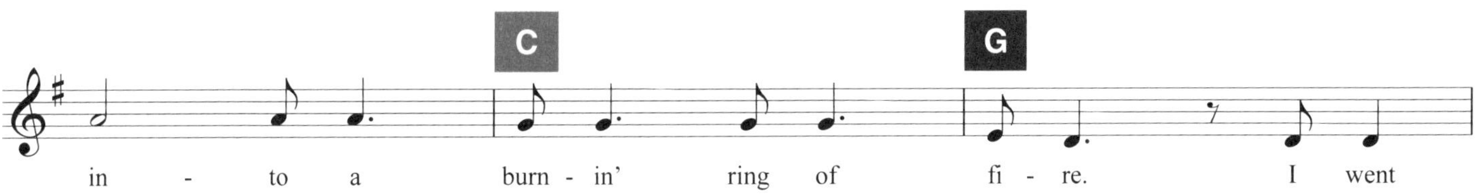

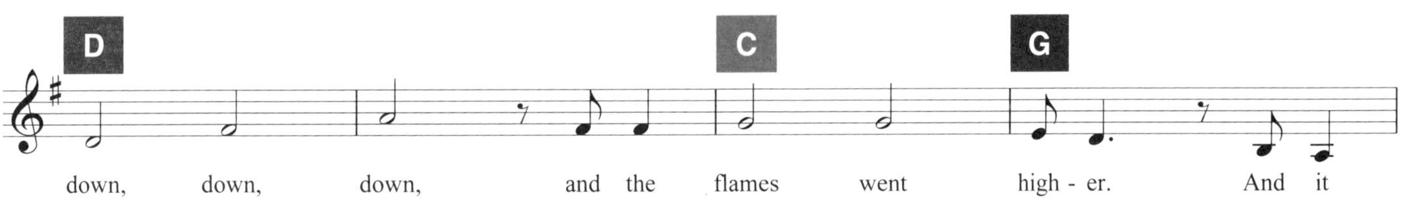

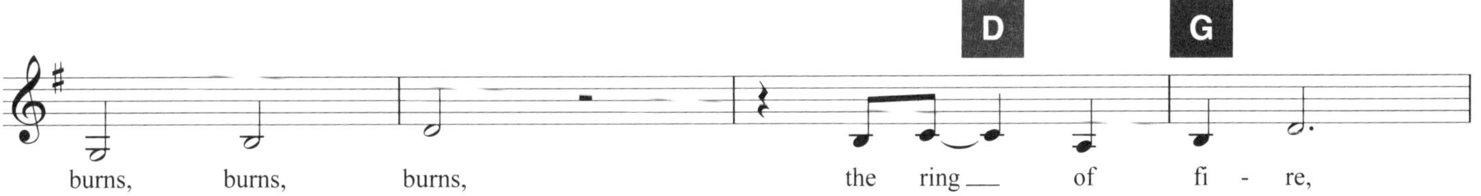

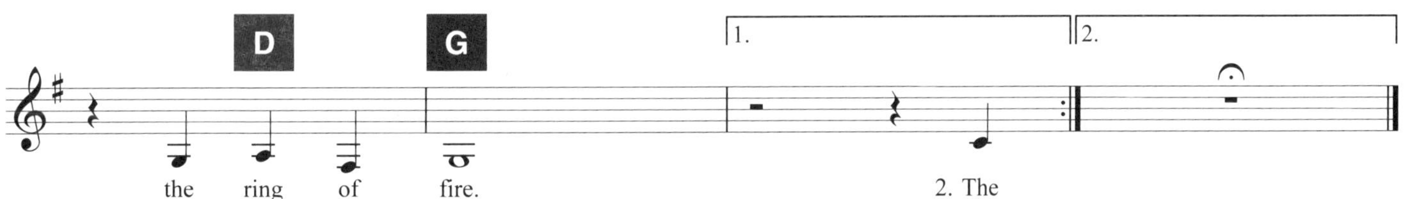

Additional Lyrics

2. The taste of love is sweet
   When hearts like ours meet.
   I fell for you like a child,
   Oh, but the fire went wild.

Streets of Bakersfield

Words and Music by Homer Joy

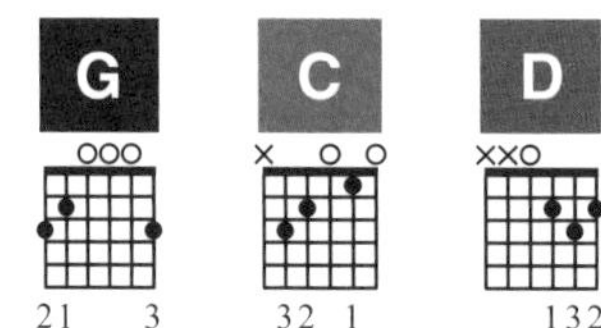

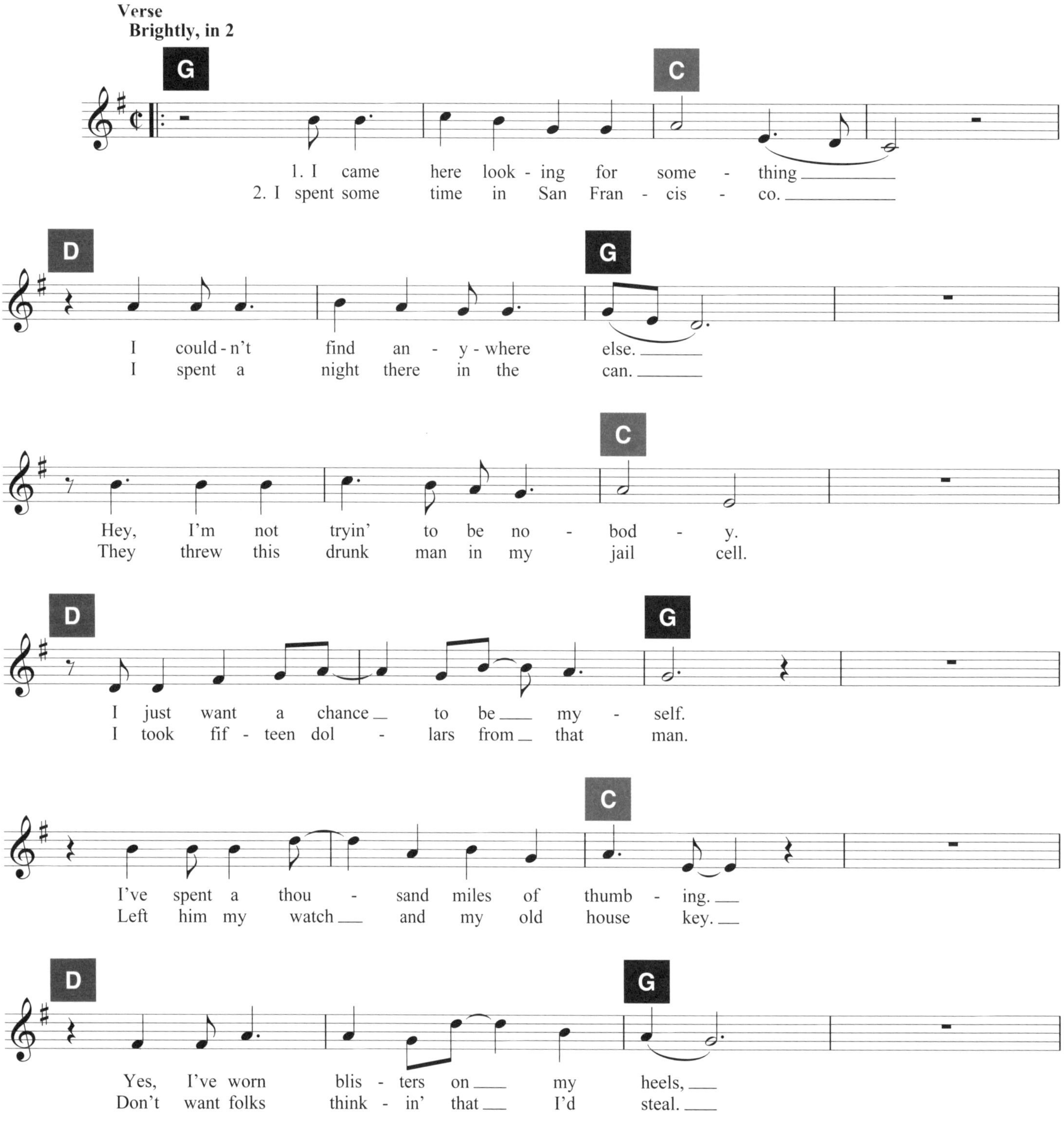

Verse

Brightly, in 2

G — C

1. I came here look - ing for some - thing
2. I spent some time in San Fran - cis - co.

D — G

I could - n't find an - y - where else.
I spent a night there in the can.

C

Hey, I'm not tryin' to be no - bod - y.
They threw this drunk man in my jail cell.

D — G

I just want a chance to be my - self.
I took fif - teen dol - lars from that man.

C

I've spent a thou - sand miles of thumb - ing.
Left him my watch and my old house key.

D — G

Yes, I've worn blis - ters on my heels,
Don't want folks think - in' that I'd steal.

C
tryin' to find me some-thing bet-ter
Then I thanked him as I was leav-ing,
D G C
here on the streets of Ba-kers-field.
and I head-ed out for Ba-kers-field.
Chorus
G C
Hey, you don't know me, but you don't like me.
D G
You say you care less how I feel.
C
But how man-y of you that sit and judge me
To Coda
D G C
2nd time, D.S. al Coda
ev-er walked the streets of Ba-kers-field.
Coda
Outro
G C
How man-y of you that sit and judge me
D G
ev-er walked the streets of Ba-kers-field.

Swing Low, Sweet Chariot

Traditional Spiritual

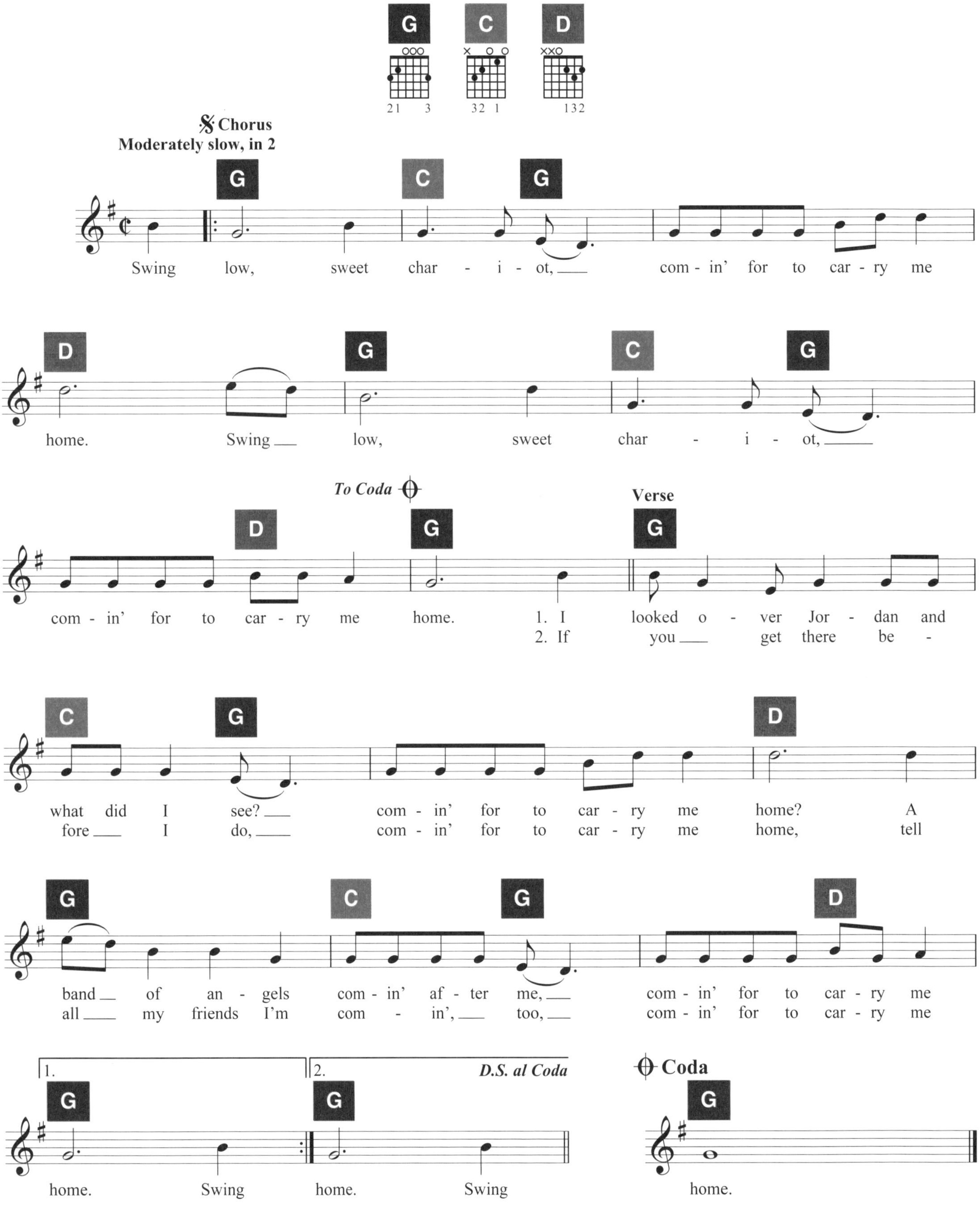

G C D

𝄋 Chorus

Moderately slow, in 2

G C G

Swing low, sweet char - i - ot, com - in' for to car - ry me

D G C G

home. Swing low, sweet char - i - ot,

To Coda 𝄌

D G

com - in' for to car - ry me home.

Verse

G

1. I looked o - ver Jor - dan and
2. If you get there be -

C G D

what did I see? com - in' for to car - ry me home? A
fore I do, com - in' for to car - ry me home, tell

G C G D

band of an - gels com - in' af - ter me, com - in' for to car - ry me
all my friends I'm com - in', too, com - in' for to car - ry me

1. G

home. Swing

2. G *D.S. al Coda*

home. Swing

𝄌 **Coda**

G

home.

A Teenager in Love

Words by Doc Pomus
Music by Mort Shuman

Additional Lyrics

2. One day I feel so happy, next day I feel so sad.
   I guess I'll learn to take the good with the bad.

3. If you want to make me cry, that won't be so hard to do.
   And if you should say goodbye, I'll still go on loving you.

This Little Light of Mine

African-American Spiritual

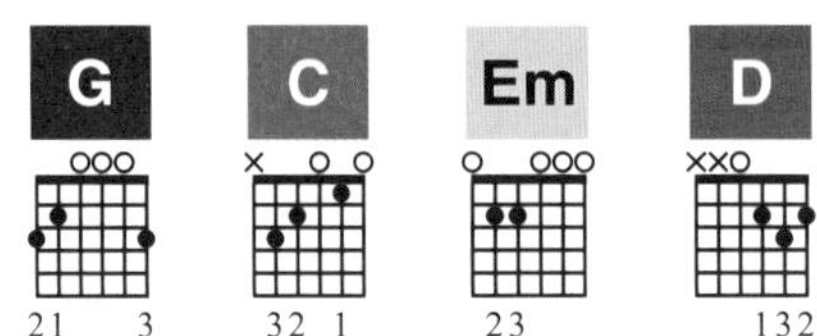

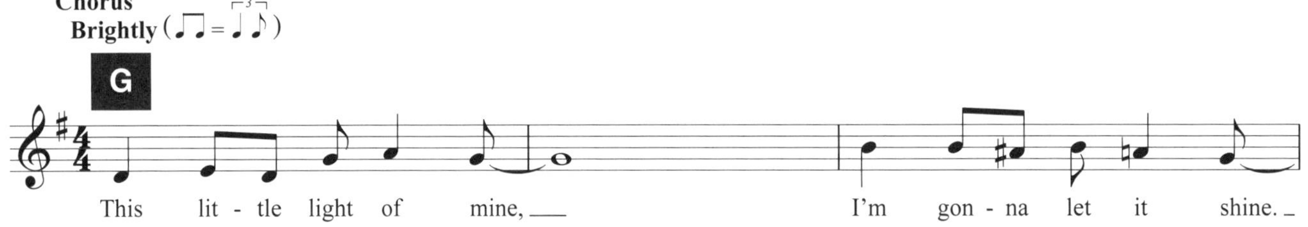

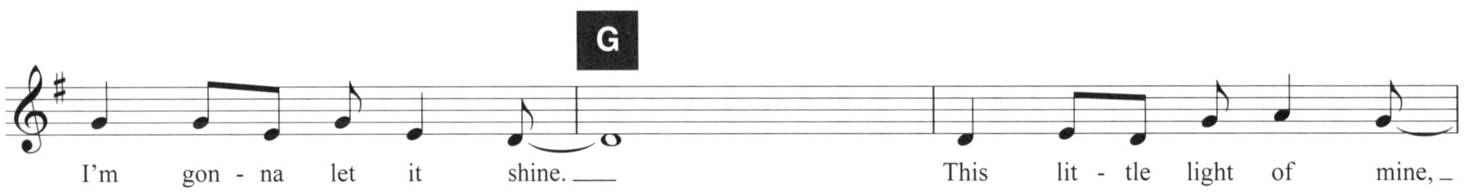

This Train

Traditional

Verse
Brightly, in 2

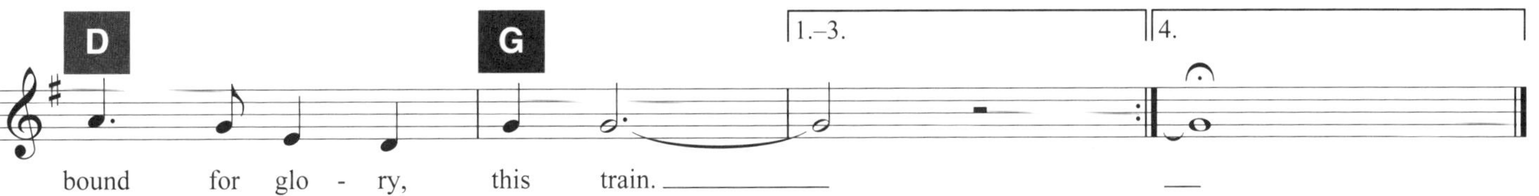

Additional Lyrics

2. This train don't carry no gamblers, this train.
   This train don't carry no gamblers, this train.
   This train don't carry no gamblers,
   No hypocrites, no midnight ramblers.
   This train is bound for glory, this train.

3. This train don't carry no liars, this train.
   This train don't carry no liars, this train.
   This train don't carry no liars,
   No hypocrites and no high flyers.
   This train is bound for glory, this train.

4. This train don't carry no rustlers, this train.
   This train don't carry no rustlers, this train.
   This train don't carry no rustlers,
   Sidestreet walkers, two-bit hustlers.
   This train is bound for glory, this train.

Travelin' Band

Words and Music by John Fogerty

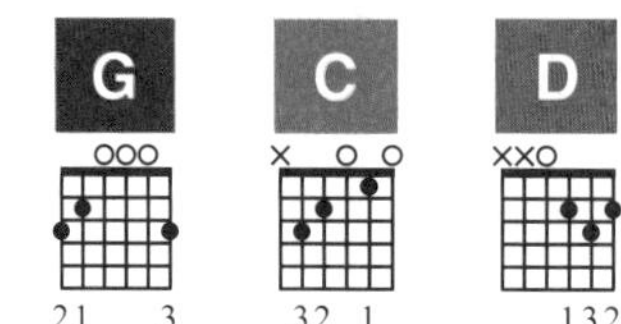

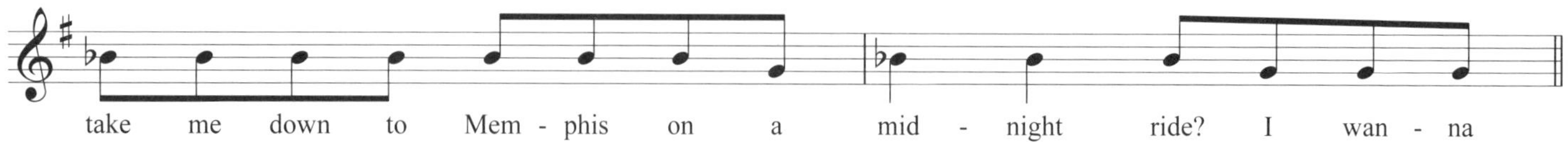

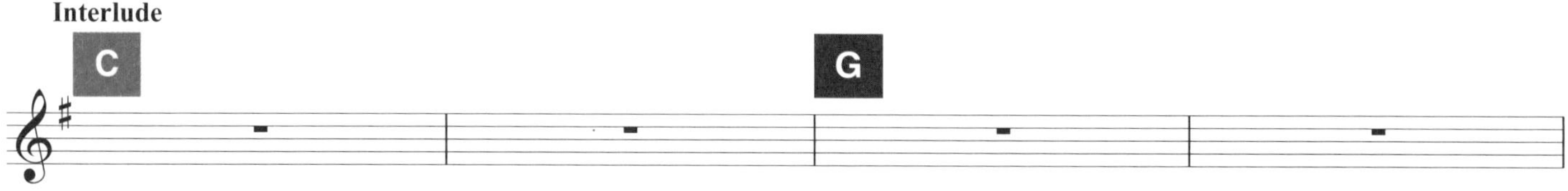

Additional Lyrics

2. Take me to the hotel, baggage gone, oh well.
   Come on, come on, won't you get me to my room?

3. Listen to the radio, talkin' 'bout the last show.
   Someone got excited, had to call the state militia.

4. Here we come again on a Saturday night
   With your fussin' and your fightin'. Won't you get me to the rhyme?

The Twist

Words and Music by Hank Ballard

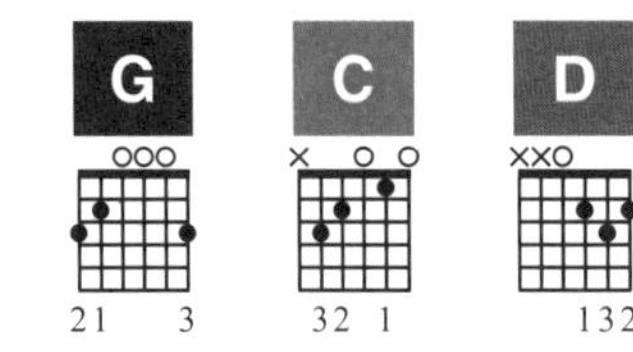

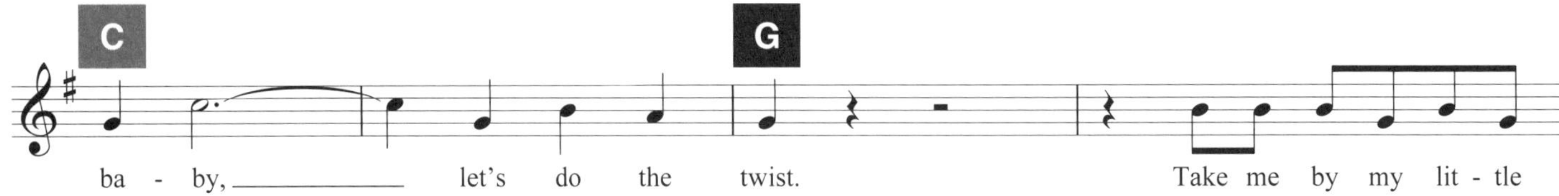

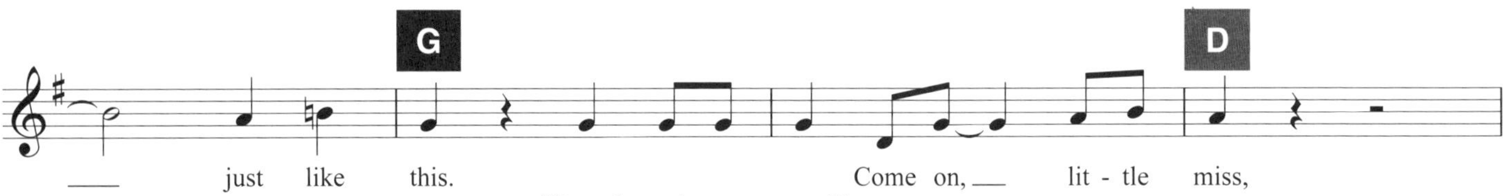

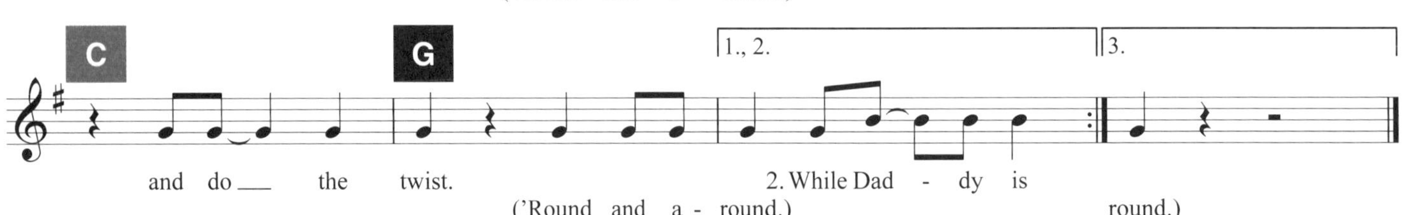

Additional Lyrics

2. While Daddy is sleeping and Mama ain't around,
   While Daddy is sleeping and Mama ain't around,
   We're gonna twisty, twisty, twisty
   Until we tear the house down.

3. You should see my little sis.
   You should see my little sis.
   She knows how to rock
   And she knows how to twist.

The Wabash Cannonball

Hobo Song

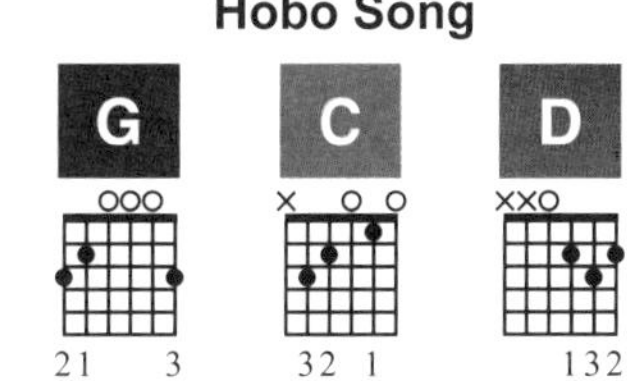

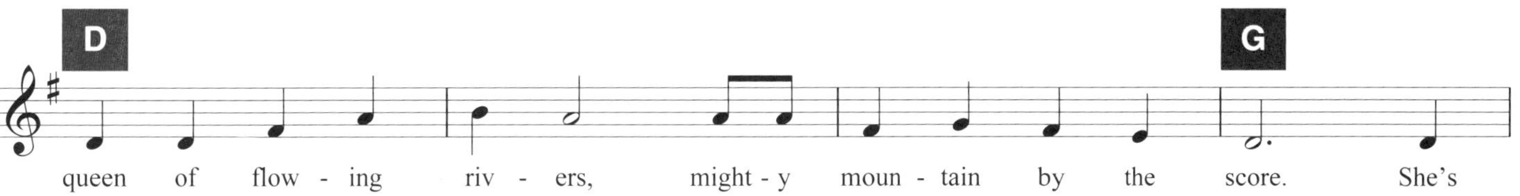

Additional Lyrics

2. Listen to the jingle, the rumble and the roar,
   Riding through the woodlands, to the hills and by the shore.
   Hear the mighty rush of the engine, hear the lonesome hobo squall,
   Riding through the jungle on the Wabash Cannonball.

3. Eastern states are dandies, so the Western people say,
   From New York to St. Louis and Chicago by the way.
   Through the hills of Minnesota where the rippling waters fall,
   No chances can be taken on the Wabash Cannonball.

4. Here's to Daddy Claxton, may his name forever stand.
   May he ever be remembered through the parts of all our land.
   When his earthly race is over and the curtain 'round him fall,
   We'll carry him to glory on the Wabash Cannonball.

Twist and Shout

Words and Music by Bert Russell and Phil Medley

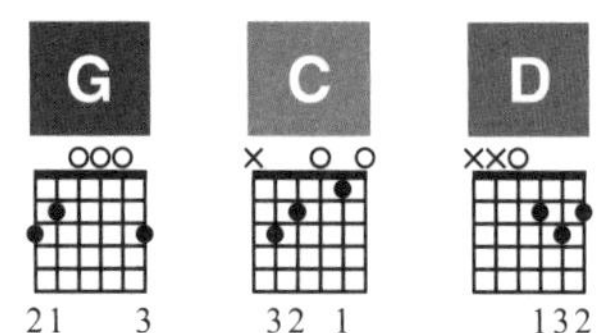

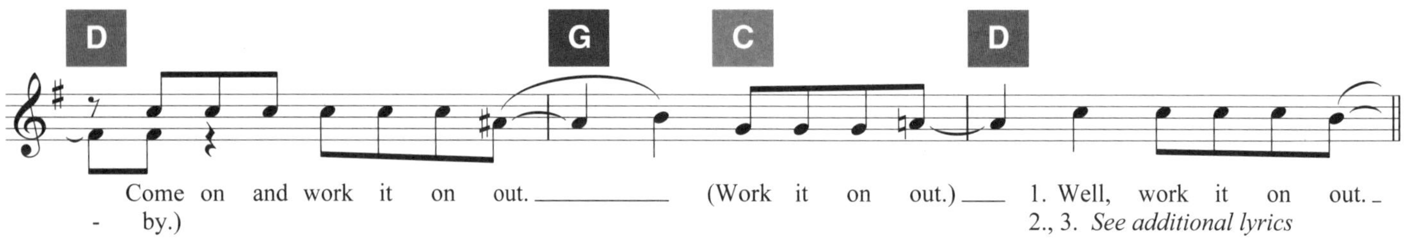

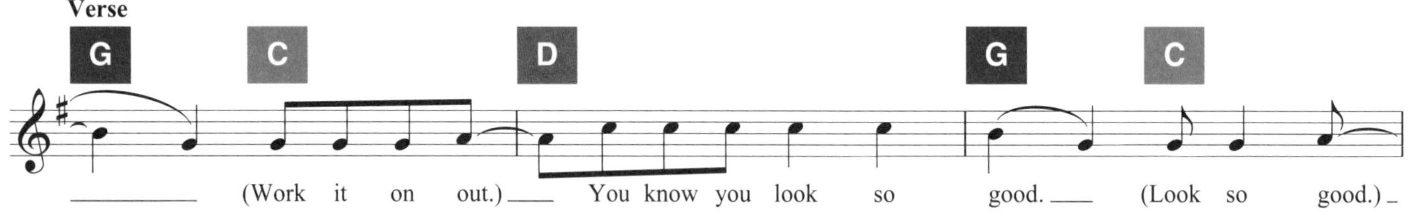

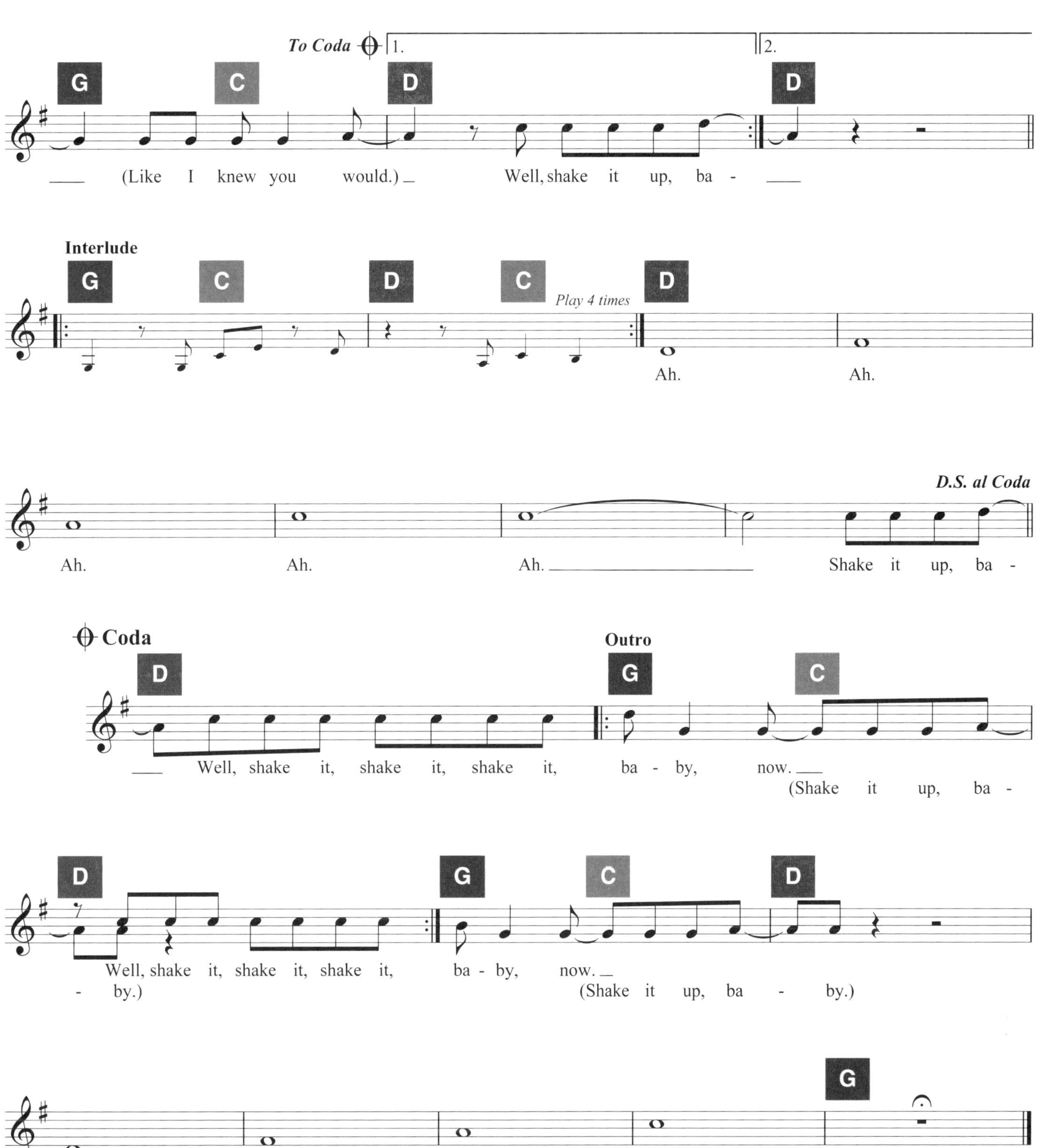

Additional Lyrics

2., 3. You know you twist, little girl, (Twist, little girl.)
You know you twist so fine. (Twist so fine.)
Come on and twist a little closer now. (Twist a little closer.)
And let me know that you're mine. (Let me know you're mine.)

When the Saints Go Marching In

Words by Katherine E. Purvis
Music by James M. Black

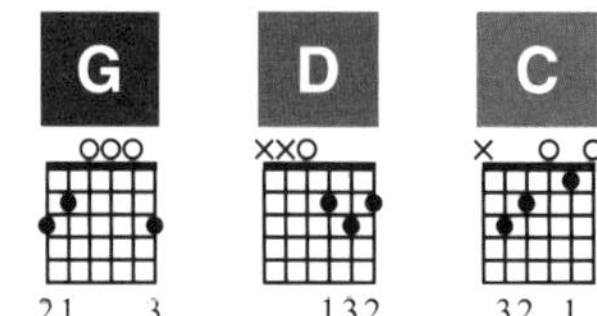

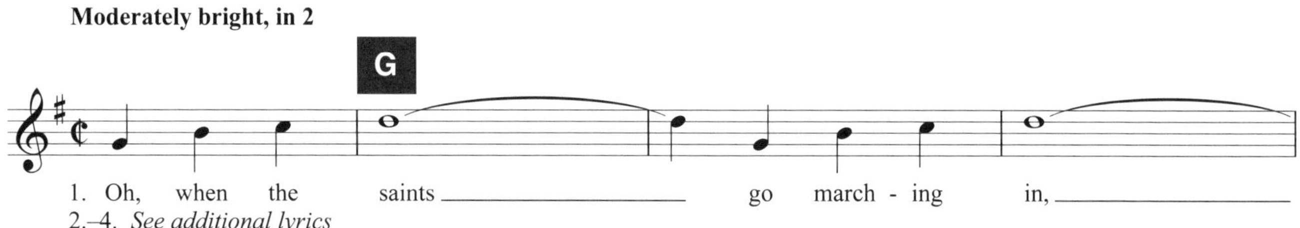

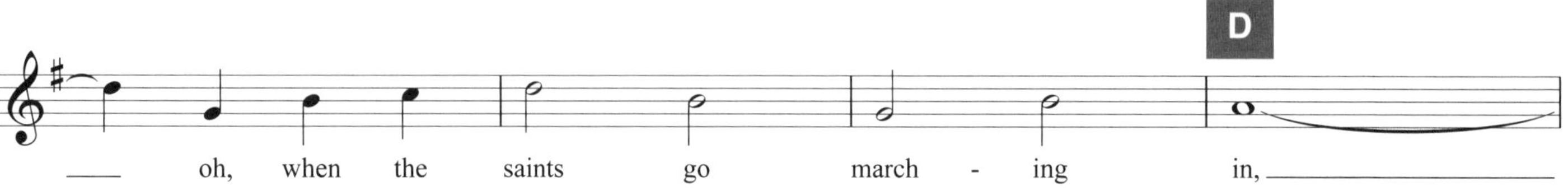

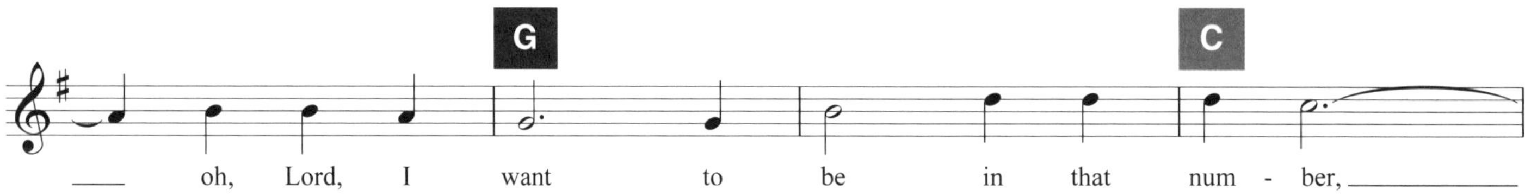

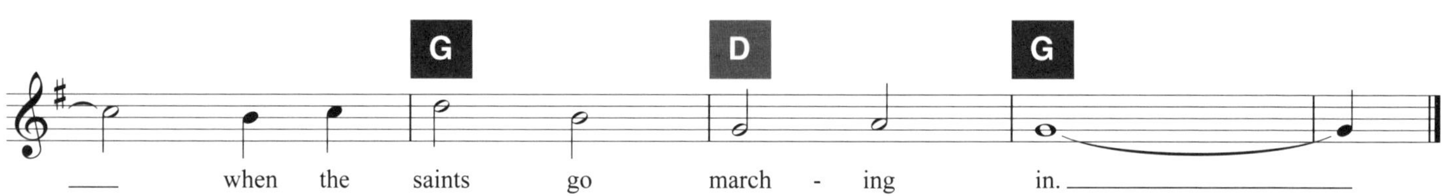

Additional Lyrics

2. Oh, when the sun refuse to shine,
Oh, when the sun refuse to shine,
Oh, Lord, I want to be in that number,
When the sun refuse to shine.

3. Oh, when the stars have disappeared,
Oh, when the stars have disappeared,
Oh, Lord, I want to be in that number,
When the stars have disappeared.

4. Oh, when the day of judgment comes,
Oh, when the day of judgment comes,
Oh, Lord, I want to be in that number,
When the day of judgment comes.

Who'll Stop the Rain

Words and Music by John Fogerty

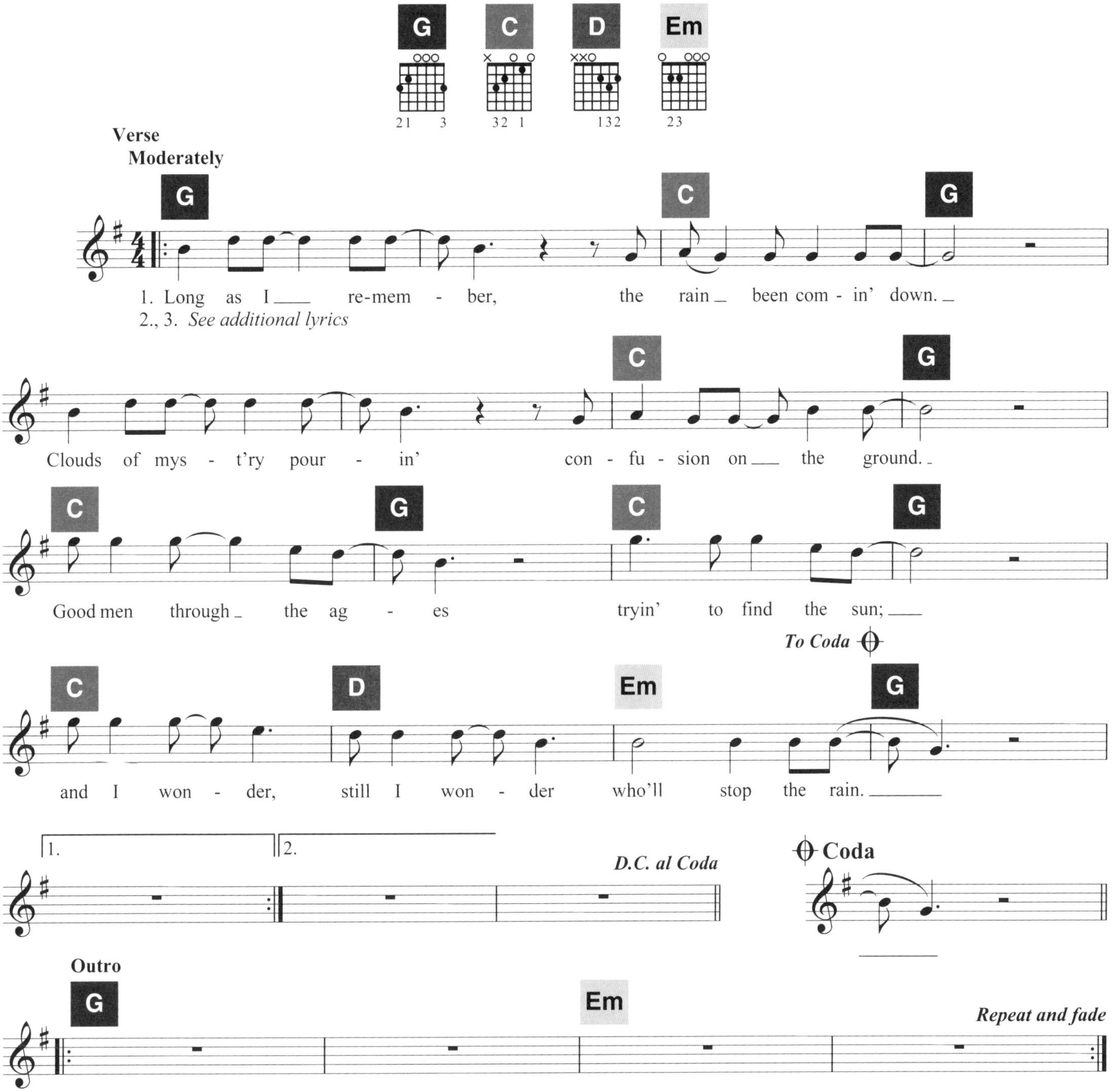

G C D Em

Verse
Moderately

G C G
1. Long as I ___ re-mem - ber, the rain _ been com - in' down. _
2., 3. *See additional lyrics*

C G
Clouds of mys - t'ry pour - in' con - fu - sion on ___ the ground. _

C G C G
Good men through _ the ag - es tryin' to find the sun; ___

To Coda

C D Em G
and I won - der, still I won - der who'll stop the rain. ___

1. 2. *D.C. al Coda*

Coda

Outro

G Em *Repeat and fade*

Additional Lyrics

2. I went down Virginia, seekin' shelter from the storm.
Caught up in the fable, I watched the tower grow.
Five-year plans and new deals wrapped in golden chains;
And I wonder, still I wonder who'll stop the rain.

3. Heard the singers playin'; how we cheered for more.
The crowd had rushed together, tryin' to keep warm.
Still the rain kept pourin', fallin' on my ears;
And I wonder, still I wonder who'll stop the rain.

Will the Circle Be Unbroken

Words by Ada R. Habershon
Music by Charles H. Gabriel

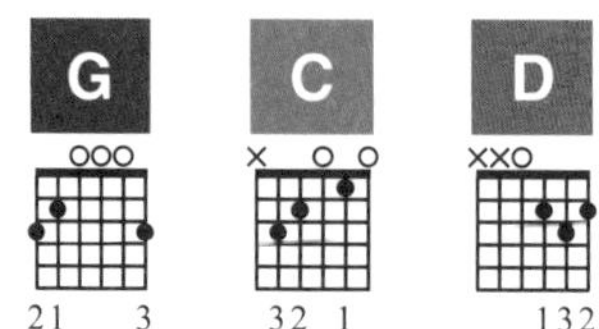

Additional Lyrics

2. Oh, I told the undertaker, "Undertaker, please drive slow,
   For this body you are hauling, Lord, I hate to see her go."

3. I will follow close behind her, try to hold up and be brave;
   But I could not hide my sorrow when they laid her in her grave.

Wooly Bully

Words and Music by Domingo Samudio

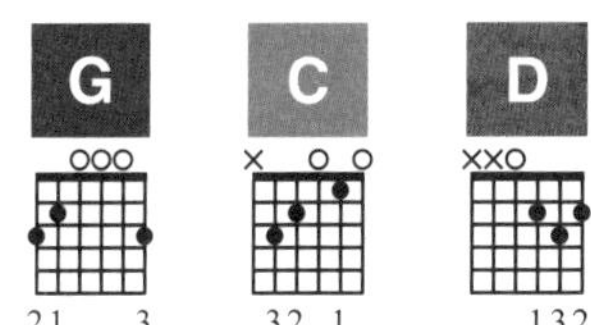

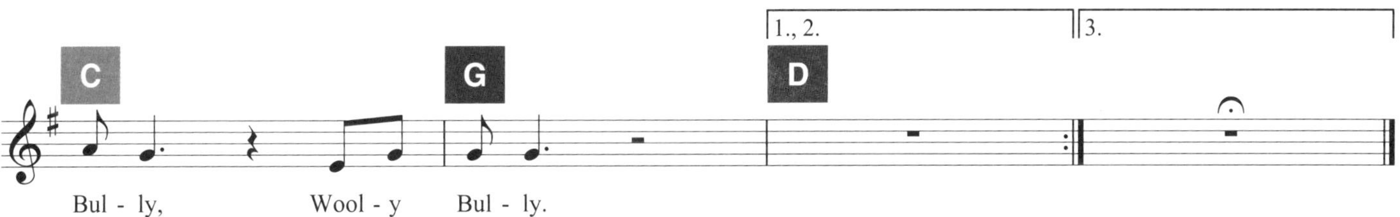

Additional Lyrics

2. Hatty told Matty,
 "Let's don't take no chance.
 Let's not be L 7.
 Come and learn to dance."

3. Matty told Hatty,
 "That's the thing to do.
 Get you someone really
 To pull the wool with you."

You Are My Sunshine

Words and Music by Jimmie Davis